God's Gangsters?

the history, language rituals, secrets and myths of South Africa's prison gangs

Heather Parker Lewis

Heather Parker Lewis

ihilihili press

Cape Town

© Heather Parker Lewis
1st edition published in 2006
2nd edition published in 2010
by ihilihili press
P.O. Box 22547
Fish Hoek 7974
Cape Town
South Africa

ISBN 978-1-920103-11-8

Cover design: Ian Strauss
Author photo: Brent Jennings
Printed and bound by Digital Action

Acknowledgements

Firstly, and in particular, I want to sincerely thank Chris Malgas from the Department of Correctional Services who is extremely wise to the ways of The Number. He has been of enormous assistance to me in completing my research over a very long period. He constantly encouraged me in my endeavours and gave willingly and unselfishly of his time after his own long and arduous working-hours. I am also deeply appreciative of the help provided by those prisoners and ex-prisoners who were prepared to share the history of The Number. Thanks and appreciation also to Lizelle Albertse and Brother Peter Hendricks. Tholakele Maphalala, who was translator and lecturer in second language teaching and multilingualism at the Centre for Applied Language at the University of Cape Town, explained the deeper meaning of the names used in The Makhulu Book of Nongoloza and was an absolute inspiration when it came to decoding Nguni words that had been corrupted by Afrikaans speaking inmates.

Heather Parker Lewis writes about people many prefer to ignore or forget — damaged and tragic individuals: street children, pimps, prostitutes, criminals, prisoners and prison gangsters. She is the author of the best selling, internationally acknowledged book *Also God's Children?... encounters with street kids* (5th Edition 2010) as well as *The Prison Speaks: Men's Voices/South African Jails* (2003) which was reviewed by Beverley Roos Muller in the Cape Argus as a book that '... *if you have strong feelings about the criminal justice system from any perspective you cannot afford to ignore. It should be made essential reading for all parliamentarians.*'

The author of *God's Gangsters?* is a qualified social worker (and estate agent!) turned writer. She graduated from the University of Cape Town in the late 1960s, later returning to teach in the School of Social Work for fifteen years. She has studied prison gangs for over ten years and this book is almost a logical conclusion to her two previous social-issue books. She is also known for her humorous business/career books: *The Good Estate Agent in South Africa; Successful Self-Publishing in South Africa; The Wannabe Writer in South Africa; The Cool, Cold Telecanvasser in South Africa* as well as a novel *The Interloper* (ihilihili press 2008). Her latest book is a biography of Olive Schreiner — rebel, writer, genius and the first emancipated woman in South Africa. When not writing she loves to garden or hike in the mountains and she is also an exponent of Bharata Natyam, South Indian temple dancing.

Foreword:

I was warned more than once when I disclosed my intention to write this book, the opinion of some warders being that I was treading on sacred territory and would pay the price. They were particularly concerned because, as a woman, I was able to recite portions of the gang *sabela* off-by-heart. Scare tactics are a great motivating factor and nothing gets done if you don't take a risk. I carried on regardless, comforting myself with the knowledge that the Number Gang members swear an oath of allegiance, not secrecy. Not one of the gang members I interviewed ever suggested I was in danger. Besides, I am a writer. I was captivated by the stories I was being told — tales of blood and violence, worlds inhabited only by men, invisible garments, vile potions and sacred stones. I was also aware that the very first person to *piemp* on the gang, tell the very secrets of The Number and expose his own followers, was Nongoloza, the gang's founding member. The Book of Twenty-Eight — *the oral history* — predicts on its final page that the secrets of the 28 Gang will be revealed by one of their own. If Nongoloza could safely confide in his warders I was confident that I could tell their story with impunity. My opinion, that the vacant post held by *tshotshisane*, the piemp, the one who squealed, is the post the absent Nongoloza himself once held, will, besides being very unpopular with 28 gang members, never be proven — but it's an interesting supposition.

I asked a senior member of the 26 Gang, "Do you too, in your hierarchy of 26, have someone who spied on the gang, betrayed the secrets of the 26s, and spilled the beans to the authorities?"

He was quick on his high horse. I was immediately informed and in no uncertain terms, "We 26s don't have *piemps* in *our* ranks!"

What makes this book special?

In *God's Gangsters?* the *sabela*, the secret coded language in which the gangs recite their oral history, rules and rituals, is presented in written form in the prison vernacular for the first time (see addendum) and translated within the text for the convenience of those who speak neither Afrikaans, Zulu nor Xhosa; at the same times the gang mythology is analysed and explored.

What motivated senior gang members to share?

I cannot say it is easy to obtain material about the gangs, but members will share for personal reasons. They may provide information to please a warder, particularly their Prison Head, if they know it will hasten their parole! My informants were inspired by the idea of a researcher who would present the facts relating to all three gangs. I have tried to live up to their belief in me and do the information they shared justice.

How did an old white grandmother gain access to previously undisclosed information?

Long-term research on street children took me into South African prisons. The information was gathered over many years: in oral form, in written form and through interviews conducted both in and out of prison and at court. My ability to access the Number Gangs developed directly from my research with *so-called*

5

rehabilitated street children. (I ran shelters for them, walked with them on the street and even got arrested with them at gunpoint!) These boys, long before their first experience of juvenile justice, had already identified with one or other of the three Number Gangs. They began to share the coded language with me, both to tease and tantalise and to test my *street credibility*. My concern was irrelevant. They were already seduced by the myths. They imagined the gangs would turn them into men.

In 2001 the Anti-Apartheid Movement extended an invitation to Denmark where I was afforded the opportunity of visiting a maximum-security prison outside Copenhagen. On my return to South Africa I had sufficient clout to offer my time voluntarily in Pollsmoor Admission Centre. There were also visits to other prisoners and prisons in the Western Cape.

Characteristics of the prison researcher?

It is all there for the asking if one is patient and perceptive and can build up a relationship of trust – which takes time – and not feel intimidated or succumb to threats. Some men will, if you question their information, threaten to withdraw their co-operation. One has to walk away from these informants and go elsewhere. It is imperative that the researcher cultivates more than one reliable source. Above all one must respect the informants and not judge them as people, but rather try to understand the choices they have made in life.

My personal stance on gangs?

I do not approve of prison gangs and I made no secret of this. I particularly dislike the bully tactics the gangs employ so that members conform minus any application of personal compassion or objective reasoning. I could not *condemn them* for what gang participation made them do, but neither could I *condone gang actions*. I believe they respected this disclosure.

📖

Obstacles?

Gang members speak in metaphors. I was cautious, taking nothing at face value and always searching for the underlying message. The gangs invent myths about each other. I learned never, ever to rely on a member from one Number Gang to provide unpolluted information about a rival Number Gang. And the members of the 28 Gang will go to amazing lengths to hide the role of the *designated women*, the so-called *wyfies*, within the gang structure. This is most likely because just about every one of the 28s has had to play this female role at some point in his prison history. Gold Card members in the 28 Gang do not provide sex for other 28s. The majority of 28s are, however, Silver Card holders and enter the gang from the left-hand side. They would probably rather die, and will certainly lie, rather than disclose their sexual status.

The most dangerous obstacle is the men's tendency to over-exaggerate. Men in prison are lonely, they will consider any outsider to be a captive audience, and they will be flattered and perform accordingly. I was told so many stories about gangsters beheading other prisoners that, if their tales had been true, there would have been cells full of decapitated victims.

I never used a tape-recorder but tried to recall as much as I could immediately after the interviews. Social workers are trained in this method. I interviewed *wyfies* and soldiers as well as the chief officers in the gangs. When they recited the *sabela* I wrote like crazy! If *they* wrote the *sabela* down then I would ask them to recite it so I could check for accuracy. If they recited it slowly I knew they were busy editing and not being honest. It is said at break-neck speed. They confided that the oral *sabela* (history, rules, rituals) was lengthy. I was impressed at the length and the complexity and in awe of men with very little education who had the ability and desire to retain so much information in their heads and who engaged for hours in polemical discussion often connected to events that, in actual fact, never even happened. There were, however, times when so much detail was supplied and in an unfamiliar language that I had to pick up a pencil. Then I occasionally encountered impatience from the interviewee. The gang members could not get their heads around the fact that I needed to take any notes at all. I had the university qualifications, many of them were barely literate and yet they *had it all* word-perfect in their heads. What, they wanted to know, was the problem with my faulty memory? In the end they decided it was because I was old and a woman.

Occasionally I sighed with irritation. I would ask a simple question and each and every time the informant would go right back to the beginning with the virtual birthing of Nongoloza and the origins of The Number. I surmised that, when the information is *only* in your head, you cannot jump in anywhere. You must return to the starting point as if you are reciting a poem or a play. And indeed often they did act out the piece — getting up, striding around, acting out all the roles with lots of expression and many hand gestures. It is magnificent drama and I enjoyed it as such — when I had sufficient time to spare. And that was seldom. We were always rushing against the clock knowing that, at any moment, the inmate could be called to lunch or summoned to return to his cell for the 3pm lock-up procedures.

There were times when I was given more information than I could handle. There were times when my information dried up and I would become frustrated. And there was the warder who could always re-motivate me with a tantalising offer of another fascinatingly tattooed source of information.

I had to listen to some very unpleasant stories. Prison is a tainted environment. I came home on occasion and wanted to scrub, not my body from top to toe, but *my mind* from inside out. I dreamed ugly dreams.

Is this book accurate?

Is this book a hundred per cent accurate? Do I have the whole story of The Number? Of course not! How boring that would be. There would be nothing left for anyone else to explore. Besides, the more they give you the less you know. Remember, this is a belief system that has been debated behind prison walls for over a century. But I have tried to present assessed facts as accurately as possible and to give all the versions. When discussing the stories of the 26 Gang with a warder he turned on me and said, "But it never happened like that! That's a lie." What he had forgotten was that *none of it* ever happened. The myths exist only inside the gang members' heads and so the story the 26 will tell is as real, for him personally, as anything a 28 will reveal. I consulted the few existing written sources and I cross-checked all my information, even information supplied by my most trusted source was suspect until verified by another.

Did Nongoloza, the so-called founder of The Number Gangs, really exist?

Nongoloza was born in 1867 and his given name was Mzozephi Mathebula. His life and lineage were well documented by the prison services. Who his real parents were – particularly his father – remains something of a mystery. Although he was reared by Nompompo and Headman Numisimani his name clearly indicates that there was doubt as to his origins. The Zulu name *Mzozephi* means: Which line (as in genealogical house) do you come from? Clearly his birth origins were in question. His name suggests that he was a foundling. Numisimani's actions suggest that he may have suspected his wife of having a baby from another man.

Who was Kilikijan founder of the 27 Gang and protector of the 26s?

There was no Kilikijan. This is a corruption of the Xhosa name *Ngilikityane* which means: The One who moved the Stone. The mispronunciation occurred because Afrikaans speaking gang members were unfamiliar with the Xhosa tongue. The word for stone in Xhosa is *ilitye* — 28 Gang myth centres around a stone on which the laws relating to same-sex practices were transcribed.

Gang, brotherhood, cult or secret society?

A gang is often described as a band of persons associating over a period of time usually for criminal purposes, working in co-ordination and frequently against mainstream beliefs. A brotherhood is an association of men that provides comradeship. A cult is a system of religious worship expressed in ritual, devotion and homage to persons or things. A secret society is kept hidden or known only to the select and has a code that adds an aura of mystery and superiority and privilege. The Number would appear to be a blend of all four possibilities but, if I were forced to choose and place The Number in a category, I would opt for cult.

Are new myths developing?

What excites me is evidence that new gang myths are indeed being created. They engage in convoluted discussions, arguing with each other, trying to make sense of aspects of gang tradition. From these debates fresh stories are emerging as well-known political figures from South Africa's early history are incorporated into The Number Gang's fantastical mythology. Millennium gang members, while they cannot be described as well educated, are certainly more literate than their predecessors and there is the widespread influence of television. There is great excitement amongst the Camp of 26 when a particular advert for a financial services house, Allan Gray Ltd., is flighted by the SABC. With the man Grey (recently linked to Sir George Grey) being acknowledged as the head of the 26 Gang, it is not impossible that, before long, the Camp of 26 (whose symbol just happens to be the dollar sign) are going to make some more outrageous claims. But more of this later in the text! I certainly expect my interpretation of new myths to be questioned.

Challenges presented when writing this book?

I had far more information than I realised when I eventually settled down to write and this had to be sorted and classified under headings. The issues I tackled were more complex and convoluted once seen on paper. I had to structure this information in a manner that would make it accessible to the general public.

There was also the difficulty of working in languages (Afrikaans/Zulu) other than my home language and translating all the material as accurately as possible without losing the essence of the story. The oral history (*Phambuka Songaqo* which Afrikaans speaking prisoners call *The Tambuka*) of the 26 and 27 Gangs, in the vernacular of the Western Cape prisons, is included as an addendum.

There was the problem of pronunciation. The Western Cape inmates had never seen anything in writing, they picked it up orally and not speaking an African language they would simplify the pronunciation. Even those fluent in Xhosa had no idea as to how some names should be spelled. Having studied Comparative African Languages at under-graduate level, one of the most exciting aspects of my research was the etymological investigation into the meaning of names of specific gang members such as Mzozephi/Nongoloza, Ngilikityane/Ntolombom, Magubaan and the original Six as well as the mythological character Pawule or Ngulugudu (possibly Nongoloza's ancestral guide). It seems no one had previously thought to follow this fascinating trail that lends such richness to the mythology of The Number. The other aspect was the use of a combination of languages in which meanings had been altered and twisted to suit the needs of The Number.

Words of caution?

It is possible that this book will encourage an avalanche of research into prison gangs. That's good. I hope it does. We still have much to learn. However, if you are tempted to go that route, two words of warning. If your informant craves publicity, says he is providing gang information but wants his name in print, be cautious, there is another agenda involved. If your informant gives you grossly inaccurate information about his own personal life, then you should not be surprised when significant portions of the rest of the information supplied turn out to be spurious. The majority of men in prison are personality disordered and possess aspects of the sociopathic personality. They live large parts of their lives in a fantasy world. They are manipulative. They have an ability to dissolve boundaries. They have plastic personalities that allow them to mould themselves to the company they keep. If you are not careful they will reflect your own history and personal aspirations right back to you. Alarm bells should ring if you are a serious researcher and your informant is going this route, because it is highly likely that the detail he is supplying about the gangs is also packed with deliberately distorted facts. And do not forget that years of heavy drug abuse will play havoc with anyone's memory.

Research issues?

I must confess that, while I tried to acknowledge the equal role of all three gangs, the 27 Gang are not as easy to tame as their 28 and 26 brothers. I did not interview any 27 brothers, but I have worked with them in a group situation and have had contact with 26s who were temporarily upgraded to the status of 27 — *vir die minute* (for the time being).

The 26 brotherhood are the easiest to access, they have no dark coital rituals to hide. To get accurate information from a 28 one must be at peace with one's sexuality and not easily intimidated. I was at an advantage in that I had access to several prisons and many different men. If I disagreed with one I could go to another. I was not going to be put in a position where a 28 member could threaten to withdraw his information if I asked questions that made him uncomfortable. Whenever information was suspect I checked it with a more reliable source.

Gold stars in the Camp of 28 are worn (tattooed) on the right shoulder, silver on the left. It's a good sign when a gang member, on introduction, proudly uncovers his shoulder and proves his position by revealing his tattooed pips or *ngunyas*.

To corroborate my own findings I consulted, for details regarding the hierarchy of the 28 Gang, both Haysom and the work of Schurink, Schurink and Lötter (a classic piece of research); for sexual exploitation of prisoners I referred to Sasha Gear et al. These texts have been written with no hidden commercial or personal agendas. I found that the only changes related to the use of nomenclature, the functions in terms of structure and roles, in the main, were unaltered.

I had an obligation. It was necessary to repeat what Haysom and Schurink et al had accomplished: if there was consistency over the last thirty years, I decided it was safe to assume that what one sees today is the same basic structure as laid down (and later reported on) by Nongoloza prior to 1900. The research that I undertook in 2005 indicates that the structure, hierarchy, the organisation of sexual roles and relationships within the 28 Gang remain unchanged since recorded independently in the 1980s by both Schurink et al and Haysom — although some errors were uncovered.

For example: Haysom lists the *mchuchisi* in the 28 Gang as *the spy*. This is incorrect. In Zulu *mchuchisi* means the public prosecutor or under-magistrate. *Ntshotshisane* from the word *ntshontsho* – a small bird or chicken – is the name of the *piemp*, the spy whose position is vacant. Haysom also refers to *Golia* – the intended name is Goliath. When recording the hierarchy in the 26 Gang he omits Nyangi One and replaces him with Landdros Number One. In relation to roles: the Draad (wireless operator) does not communicate with other gangs but only records and returns to report to his own camp.

The main motives for writing God's Gangsters?

Firstly, I wanted to capture the mythology while it was still being recited. I was already aware of changes in presentation, with the members who had been in prison longest relying far more on Xhosa and Zulu during interviews. Secondly, the Number Gang story is also part of South African history, it is not a history of which one can be proud, but it deserves to be recorded. Thirdly, the uncontrolled growth of the prison gangs has resulted in spiralling crime figures in South Africa. I am still hoping that one day the Department of Correctional Services will read *God's Gangsters?* and recognise the existence of the Number that runs the entire prison system as well as the staff and volunteers (churches included) that work in prisons. If the Department of Correctional Services were able to introduce a genuine rehabilitation programme in South African prisons and do something about rape and stop the easy availability of drugs, instead of using gang members to keep law and order (thereby acknowledging their authority over all prisoners) it is just possible we might see a reduction in violent crime. Many men, because of the inadequate systems operating in jails, are raped in prison or are coerced into providing sex and once released they reclaim their manhood by raping women and children. But Correctional Services judge their efficacy by one single criterion. If there are no prison riots they must be doing a good job!

Are prison gangs changing and on the move?

The Number Gangs are accommodating and, with some 90% of prisoners being released, it is inevitable that The Number (through its released members) should see the value of making a play for power and control of the drug market and illegal abalone market once back in society. Outside of prison the 28 Gang align themselves with The Firm and the 26 Gang with The Americans. Inside prison gang members constantly bewail the fact that The Number is no longer true to its roots, that the discipline is lax, that there are now soft options, that young upstarts no longer respect senior members. There is a realisation amongst gang members that they are being used as pawns, while a few elite are making a lot of money and getting the benefit from the drugs that are sold in prison. Many gang members are unhappy with those men, recruited outside of the prisons, entering the prison system with rank. (They ignore the fact that originally *all* the Number Gang members were recruited on the outside and that during the early days, when members were imprisoned, some men would have been recruited outside and others inside prison and right from the start, human nature being what it is, there would probably have been conflict over interpretation of gang law.) Since the 1980s the 27 Gang has been declining in numbers; since 1994 (with rights for all) the Gold Line (Fighting Line) of the 28 Gang has played a less active role. At some Admission Centres, through which awaiting-trial prisoners must be processed, the Gold Line has been closed. And, because of declining numbers in the Camp of 27, the Camp of 26 are arguing to alter gang protocol so that they can engage directly with the Camp of 28 without having to go through a 27 as an intermediary.

The oldest of the gangs is the 28 Gang. Both the Gang of 28 and the Gang of 27 began their existence outside of prison some time in the late 1880s early 1890s. The 26 Gang was formed in the 1900s and is the only branch of The Number to have originated inside prison.

Part One –The World Outside

1. **Mzozephi Mathebula:** p17 – the early years, from his birth in 1867; with a mention of his death in 1948.

2. **Number Gangs:** p19 – a basic introduction to the three Number Gangs, their history, development from the 1880s and adaptability; mention of other prison gangs (p20); rationale for The Number's existence (p21); the Makhulu Book (p24).

3. **Historicity:** p29 – historical events, from 1600 to the end of the Anglo-Boer War, that impacted on the life of Mzozephi.

4. **Bad Boy to Brigand:** p33 – the development of Mzozephi's criminal career during early adulthood; he joins the brigands at Klipriversberg (p34).

5. **Nongoloza:** p35 – Mzozephi becomes Nongoloza/Nongoloza's personal attributes in adulthood; a list of significant names in the story of The Number (p36); the banishing of women & the Regiment of the Hills (p37); Nongoloza's written comment on how he structured his original gang (pp37-38); *abathelisa* (p38); characteristics of the Makhulu Book (p39); the negative identity (p40).

6. **The Ninevites:** p41 – Nahum and the bible; Nongoloza discloses about the Ninevites (p42); his bitterness (p43); 1908: prison, escape, re-arrest, indeterminate sentence (p43); Ntlokonkhulu (p44); gangs defeated (p44); no one knows the origin of the name The Number Gangs (p44); revolution in the ranks and the meaning of the name Ngilikityane (p45); The Crossroads (p46); Magubaan (pp46-47); Number 27 and the relationship between Nongoloza and Ngilikityane (p47); Number 26 and the symbolic meaning of the names of the original six (pp47-49); Ngilikityane had reasons (p50); Grey (p50); Sir George Grey (pp51-52).

7. **Witbene:** p53 – the gangs spread across the prison spectrum; warder Paskin (p53); Nongoloza discloses why he capitulates (p54); defeat, recidivism and death (p54); buffalo thorn tree (p55).

Part Two – The World Inside

8. **Potent Cocktail:** p59 – details of the symbols that differentiate between the gangs; gang language (p59-60); symbols and flags (p61); tattoos and the significance of Moliva Boy and the *heart beats twice* for the 28s, *water* and other sexual terminology in the 28 Gang (pp62-63); the mines (p64); *the shotgun* (p64).

9. **Eight until Late:** p65 – the 28 Gang & the analysis of structure, hierarchy, uniforms, roles; sex wars/issues (p66); origin of Amasilva (p67); re-opening the Gold Line (p67); sexual practices and partners/attitude of Correctional officers (pp70 -74); accessing the 28s' clothing cupboard (p75-80); release from prison and returning of the invisible uniform (p80).

10. **Sixes and Sevens:** p81– the 26 Gang; initiation (p89); oath of 26 (p92); Madakeni's speech (p93); Nogidela's speech (p94); special events (pp95-97); human rights (pp98-99); punishments (pp100-103); founder members (p103); human sacrifices? (pp103-104); the real Ngilikityane? (pp104-106).

Part Three – The World Within

11. Nongoloza's Book: p109 exploration of myths and the Book of Beliefs; Hitler (p113); important dates for The Number (p113); understanding the relevance of The Crossroads (p114); literary style adopted in the story of The Crossroads, semantics, gang language, Zulu origins/vocabulary (pp115-117); The Crossroads in translation (pp118-124); The 28s' version of The Crossroads (p125); the Huistoe Kom or Homecoming of The Number gangs (p126); the Homecoming of the Camp of 28 plus a translation (pp127-132); the Homecoming of the Camp of 26 in translation (pp132-133); why The Number succeeds (pp134-135).

14

Part One
the world outside

Umzakwaan: members of The Number are encouraged to view their lives outside of the prison walls as the umzakwaan – one small moment in time – a period of little significance.

Mzozephi: the word *umzi* forms the stem of Mzozephi's name and *umzi* means a house in Zulu, but in this case *a house* as in *genealogical lineage* while the suffix *phi?* - the interrogative - gives us the meaning 'from what house does he come?' or 'who exactly is he descended from?' In 1887, at the age of twenty *Mzozephi Mathebula* took the name of *Jan Note* - an Afrikaans name. By 1897, when he was thirty years old and the leader of a gang of brigands, he was called *Nongoloza* (The Giver of Rules) by his followers.

The Number Gangs: the name evolved over many years; originally they were known as *The Regiment of the Hills* or *Umkosi wa Ntaba* and then as *The Ninevites*, a name used in prison even after the First World War; some bands of vagrants who owed allegiance were called *Nongoloza*; in prison they were *Ninevites* and *People of the Stone* and sometimes *Amalitas* (from *ilitye* or stone in the the Nguni languages); the 26s and 27s were also known as *The Scotlanders*. The latter worked with money — usually other people's money! It is not known for certain how the term *The Number* originated or what it was based on.

Chapter One

Mzozephi Mathebula

the birth, life, career and death of the man whose energy, charisma, aggression and negative vision gave us the Number Gangs

a legend in his lifetime

Mzozephi Mathebula was born in the year 1867 in a kraal nestling within the plump green hills of the Land of the Zulu. His arrival seems to have occasioned a degree of surprise. Children in the Nguni culture are given names relating to their birth circumstances and Nompompo, whose name means *the tap* or *the pump*, senior wife of Headman Numisimani, bestowed upon this baby a name with the literal meaning of: *Where did you spring from?*

The name *Mzozephi* leads one to suspect that this may have been a foundling child, the baby of a young unmarried woman of the clan, because the name raises questions regarding the boy's parentage and, more significantly, whose ancestors he should be honouring.

Certainly Headman Numisimani was not impressed and, although the child was allowed to assume the clan name of Mathebula, it was not long before Nompompo, accompanied by Mzozephi and the rest of her brood, was banished to the farm of Tom Porter, a place where the Tugela River takes its course from the mighty Drakensberg Mountains.

From all accounts Mzozephi was not an easy child to rear. His early reputation indicates that there were problems during adolescence and he left his mother's homestead in his mid-teens.

Mzozephi was described by those who met him as short and stocky with piercing eyes. He made up for his lack of physical stature with his astuteness, intelligence, creativity, cunning and stealth.

He soon put his skills to use as a career criminal.

By the time Mzozephi died in 1948 at the age of 81 years, he had been witness to the demise of the Zulu nation, the defeat of the Boer Republics and the formation of the Union of South Africa under a central national government that contrived to exclude the majority of the population.

With the unification of South Africa the prisons became a national matter under a newly created central government. To these prisons Mzozephi – in his role as Nongoloza, King of the Bandits – bequeathed, much like the wicked fairy Carabosse, an unsolicited legacy, the prison Number Gangs and their aftermath.

His legacy has outlasted the British Empire, survived the Apartheid System and continues to flourish in the prisons of the Department of Correctional Services of the Republic of South Africa well into the New Millennium.

He would be *Inkosi Kakhulu*, the Great Chief, for the rest of time!

Chapter Two

The Number Gangs

an introduction to The Number Gangs and a comment on what makes them different from prison gangs in other countries

26, 27, 28

The Number Gangs operating in South African prisons have roots that are deeply embedded in the early history of this country. Their origins go back to the 1880s — to the days of President Paul Kruger and the old Transvaal Republic and the colonisation of Zululand and Natal.

The values that bind the Number Gangs – the historical codes that keep them, the structure that ensures their survival – have hardly altered in over one hundred years.

The Number (although at the time it was known by a different name) existed prior to the amalgamation of the four provinces into the Union of South Africa in 1910. When South Africa was declared a Republic in the 1960s and a Democracy in 1994, warders and prisoners noted that ...*these external political events have no bearing on The Number and the way the gangs control the prisons of this country.*

As early as 1912 the South African parliament was addressed on the issue of the prison gangs. The Department of Prisons held meetings with all prison heads and proposed that gang membership be declared a punishable offence and gang leaders be incarcerated on Robben Island. By 1914 the Minister of Justice was declaring that the State had *everything under control*. At an Imbizo in 2002, at Pollsmoor Admission Centre outside Cape Town, the Minister of Correctional Services made an identical statement, despite compelling evidence to the contrary.

The Number consists of the 26s, 27s and 28s. The 28 Gang is the oldest of the Number Gangs. Both the 28 and 27 Gang developed outside of prison some time in the 1880s. The 26 Gang is the only one of the three Number Gangs to have its origins in the prison system itself and this occurred in about 1907 or 1908. We can be reasonably sure of these dates because early prison records inform us as to when the gang leaders were arrested and where they were incarcerated.

To put it at its simplest: the 26 Gang specialises in robbery and smuggling (*kroon/money*), through acts of cunning they *keep the jail alive*; the 28 Gang in sex (*gif/poison*) and violence; the 27s (*manskap van bloed/men of blood*) can be classified as career criminals specialising in deeds of aggression. Whilst maintaining a symbiotic relationship with the 26s, the Gang of 27 simultaneously monitors and enforces and protects the laws and codes of The Number and negotiates with the 28s on behalf of the 26 Gang. The analogy is obvious, when a man goes to prison the present Department of Correctional Services will categorise his criminal profile according to whether he has committed an economic offence (robbery/fraud), a sexual offence, or a crime of violence.

There are other gangs in prison that claim Number status: the 29s, or Desperadoes and the 25s, the prison *piemps*, who collaborate with warders for gain, but neither are considered part of the original, legitimate Number stock. The Air Force Gang – who organise mass escapes – have no connection to the Number Gangs although they have been heavily influenced by their terminology, strategies and structure.

The Number exists as an abnormal counter-culture within the prison system, a counter-culture in which the 28 Gang has the power to transform heterosexual men into women for the duration of their stay in prison — because sex, like drugs, is viewed as *just another commodity*. It is a culture that works in direct opposition to any meaningful rehabilitation efforts that would adversely influence the gangs' performance in terms of running illicit drug syndicates in South African prisons.

Members of the Number Gangs, however, have a very different perception of their role within the prisons and tend to romanticise their origins. But it's a cover-up, a whitewashing of the truth.

New initiates are led to believe the gang is there to protect them, care for them and that joining is voluntary. When they discover the truth it is too late. Nominally recruits choose to join, but no one leaves The Number of their own volition.

My informant – clad in a neon-orange uniform stamped all over with the word *prisoner* – was, in part, proud of the gang's image and its achievements and clearly he idolized the senior ranking members.

"The Number is necessary," he emphasized. Then he added an aside, "But remember, the first thing you have to understand is — it's not a gang!" He was insistent, "The Numbers were there to improve prison conditions and they did improve their (inmates) miserable existence and that was the original intention. It was in the apartheid days, and long ago, to work against the *boere* who oppressed the prisoners."

He passed a hand over his face and frowned, "I can't think of the English word." He almost smiled and his body inclined in my direction, "*Wetslaaners*, that's what they were — to see prisoners got their rights, to get what they needed and was rightly theirs." He leaned closer, pressed his hands together with thumbs extended. Then he bent his head, thumb tips against his lips. "You see," he confided, speaking softly and slowly, "it was like this. Nongoloza, he started The Numbers, and this was a very, very long time back. And he was working in the prison kitchen, and they had to see that the food was properly cooked – with care – not just thrown together any old how as the warders would do it, but cooked properly and with salt and that added. So the Number started to make sure things were done properly for the prisoners, because in those days nobody cared and prisoners were starved and beaten and there was no such thing as human rights. And, of course, those early members, they were all black Africans."

I wanted to argue, because I was pretty sure it was not quite like that, if at all. But I kept my mouth shut. He was not providing facts, but rather a symbolic story; it was up to me to translate the symbolism. He was speaking in metaphors and parables to assist me with the concepts, very much as Nongoloza would have addressed his band of unsophisticated brigands.

I was fascinated. He was interpreting The Number as a *belief system and human rights organisation* for prison inmates, an early version of the African Renaissance!

Suddenly, unexpectedly, he shared his disenchantment, his speech coming in staccato bursts, "That's how it started. As a benefit for the prisoners. But things have changed. Especially lately. It's not run properly like it was intended. Things went wrong with Coloureds joining and even Whites." He was quite disgusted, "*That* was never meant to be!" He continued, "In the old days nobody could just become a member of The Number. You had to prove yourself, go through initiation. Now, these days, if a man comes to jail who deals drugs on the outside then the very next day, he's a *Number*. That isn't the way it was. It was to benefit prisoners and also to see that men in prison treated each other with a certain respect, because the warders, they didn't care about that. Now there are rules for just about everything and God help those who step out of line. And if they get beaten as a gang punishment, like happened to two guys this morning, then the warders keep out of it. It's gang stuff and if prisoners want to be involved they must take what goes with it. There is no protection from the warders. Also, they are scared, because the gang could get them later if they interfere. Or get their families. It just takes one phone call. That's all."

He gave a fatalistic shrug — end of story.

Changing direction he described how to treat a fever in prison, "Walk up and down. Never lie down. And drink, all day. Lots of water and tea all the time."

I thanked him for the advice, both medical and metaphorical. The interview was over.

I was intrigued and amused by his blatantly racist comments. The Number has, historically speaking, always been viewed as a non-racial organisation. Anyone could join. His comments recalled the prejudice expressed at many an all-white-post-democracy dinner party with guests being encouraged to dissect transformation and Black Economic Empowerment!

I was told more than once that the idea behind The Number was to protect fellow prisoners against warders, to help improve prison conditions, to encourage prisoners to be disciplined, to respect each other, to care about each other and not fight amongst themselves because *warders don't care how prisoners handle each other*. The gang members believe chaos would ensue if there were no gangs to keep order. They see themselves as exerting some control in the face of the warders' attitude of *don't care*.

On many occasions men spoke nostalgically of a time when The Number was pure.

I was lectured, "The Number is in a state of flux. With the 28s and 26s operating in the community, far-reaching changes, damaging to the gangs' original intentions, are being made. The strict codes of behaviour are no longer being applied. Men are promoted without any merit or the knowledge they need and men are being initiated into The Number outside of prison."

What I was being told was, of course, part fact and part fantasy.

The original bandits under Nongoloza were plunderers and highway robbers. They were thieves who preyed on their own people – the poorest of the poor – black migrant-labourers returning from the mines to their kraals. There are vivid descriptions (in newspapers of the time) of farm raids with beasts left to die slow, horrible deaths – chunks of flesh ripped from their haunches – while the bandits enjoyed a feast of roast beef.

Secondly, the movement began outside of prison and with the opening of South Africa's borders and an increase in the drug trade, it has acted opportunistically. Both the 26 Gang (acting as The Americans) and the 28 Gang (acting as The Firm) are once again involved in communities beyond the prison walls.

Thirdly, the Number Gangs have always accommodated to changing circumstance. It's one of their strengths.

Although it must be accepted that the gangs offer their members status and some protection from ad hoc physical violence and sexual exploitation, The Number can best be envisaged as a *living entity* and its members little more than worker ants who are there to sustain The Number and keep it alive.

Gang members are discouraged from asking awkward questions. They cannot think or act for themselves. Their first duty is always to The Number and once they become members their every act and thought is monitored. The application of logic is not encouraged.

They've always been a bad lot with a first-class public relations officer!

Most Number Gang members will be 26s or 28s and, in terms of membership, the 28s will always claim a majority. They pride themselves on being the strongest, oldest, biggest gang.

It is said that only about fifteen out of every hundred gang members will have the status of a 27.

The 26 Gang boasts about its exclusivity. As they see it, anyone can provide the sex that the 28s are seeking. The skills required in the 26 Gang are more specialised and the restrictions placed on members in terms of sexual exploits stringent. Men who have been sodomised can never become 26s or 27s. They are considered contaminated. The 26s adopt an aggressive stance towards sodomy, but not out of the kindness of their hearts. With every rape a potential candidate is lost to the gang. But that is not to say 26 Gang members do not risk being excommunicated when they indulge in same-sex practices on the sly.

Members of The Number refer frequently to *The Book of Twenty-Six* or *The Book of Twenty-Eight*. These 'books' – also called *Makhulu Book* (big book) – are not in any written, tangible form, but have been handed down orally from one generation of inmates to the next. They are memorised – to be repeated to the letter when required – and cover the history of the gangs, the codes, rules, laws, regulations, punishment rituals, structure (judicial, civil and military), hierarchy, uniforms, insignia, roles of each rank and even *drillbaan* – the specific instructions for the drilling of the soldiers – as well as detailed instructions on how, when and where the leadership of the three branches of The Number may meet to communicate with each other.

The compulsory learning of *The Book* takes up much time in prison, prevents the gang members from concentrating on any other form of study and is the focal point of their indoctrination into what can well be viewed as a cult. If they spent less time on *The Book* and applied to further their education they would all come out of prison with matriculation certificates.

If any member is unable to recite his portion of *The Book* accurately he will, after three days, be given a dressing-down and demoted.

The difference between the Number Gangs in South Africa and prison gangs in other parts of the world is that, in South Africa, the prison gangs have created their own reality, a system that exists within the prisons which has an idiosyncratic history, a coded language referred to as *sabela* or *salazisa* – a blend of Afrikaans and African Nguni languages – roles, rules, rituals, mythologies and even invisible clothes which only the initiated can identify. They are supremely powerful and they run the lives of all the inmates. The gangs operate totally independently of each other in terms of teaching, training, disciplining members and in managing the affairs relating to each gang. Each branch of The Number has its own revered leader, parliament, symbol, salute and flag but, because The Number was the brainchild of one man, Mzozephi Mathebula (alias Nongoloza), all three gangs share common roots.

Each section adheres to a quasi-military structure with a political-judicial component. Ranks and titles resemble those in the British Army: there is a Governor General who rules and a *Boer Vecht Generaal* who fights (in imitation of the Cape Colony and the Anglo-Boer War) and a doctor who examines new recruits and determines their fitness for specific positions in the gangs. The judicial system is identical to that found in any Western court of law: there is the judge, magistrate, prosecutor and clerk.

Not everyone in the prison system is a gang member – abstaining out of choice or due to lack of eligibility – but there is no prisoner or warder who is not directly affected by the activities of the Number Gangs.

There is no such thing as a *skone frans*, an innocent prisoner not involved in gang activity. In some way every single man is manipulated or intimidated into making his contribution even if he is never taken through the ritual of initiation. If The Number allowed individual prisoners to escape their influence they would lose the power base that fuels their existence. The gang code states ...*you will tell a frans twice and if he does not listen then the third time the gang will teach you how to deal with him.*

When commodities are scarce, when gang members insult each other, when the responsibilities given to each of the three gangs are not carried out according to the code and rules, then hostility will break out between the gangs as boundaries are breached and etiquette ignored.

A seemingly minor breach can start a war.

My next informant was an elderly man. He had been out of prison for some years and had converted to Christianity. But in prison he was a ranking member of the 26s and he had the tattoos to prove his status.

He explained: "You can't just ask anybody his rank when they arrive in prison. That's undiplomatic. The lines of authority are very structured and it must be so or there's woerwaai (chaos). In the late nineteen-nineties, at Medium A Prison at Pollsmoor, there were no 27s. A new inmate, a *stimela* (someone transferred from another prison), arrived and it's normal for a 27 to go to the *stimela* (train) and ask what gang he belongs to and then the 27 reports back, first to the 28s and then to the 26s. Because Nongoloza (the 28) he never approaches danger first. The stimela follows protocol and stands at the toilet, which is neutral territory, and the 28s watch while the '6s and '7s spin the Number. When no 27 is available, and nowadays there are not many, then a 26 can become a 27 for the moment. Now the 26 in his role as Hollander, in this instance, he went to the new inmate and, instead of passing on the information to the 28s, he went first to the 26s, because his Blackboard, his teacher, was negligent and had not taught him properly. And that sparked a war. Something small as that, disrespect for Nongoloza, started a gang war!"

One can almost think of each gang as a separate country. One gang will not interfere with the internal policy and decision making of another gang unless those internal policy-decisions threaten to destabilize the boundaries around the system. The system has been designed to allow for maximum co-operation between the gangs so that the overall aim – the survival of The Number as an almost separate, sentient, living organism – is attained. And, with this in mind, the Makhulu Book, prescribes for every contingency.

The 28s, being the oldest most established gang, are given two days of the week, from Saturday to Sunday, to carry out their business. On Friday (Rantsoenjaar) or Ration Day the Colonel of the Gold Line/Bloodline sends out instructions and on the Saturday the members carry out whatever instructions have been given and the gang *downs* (in their parliament) over the *wrongs* committed. On Sunday the new recruits are initiated, but only after the other Camps/Gangs have been duly informed. On this day the soldiers of the 28s also *down* – as in deal with any business that has come their way. The other two Camps get one day a week to complete their work.

Members believe in The Number and follow the codes that keep it as steadfastly as adherents of a fundamentalist religion. During the initiation ritual, which follows on from The Homecoming, the member will embrace The Number as his *only* family. In fact there is a lot of social control going on in the gang. It is almost entirely about mind power games and members watch and monitor and report on each other at every opportunity.

It happens in all cults.

📖

Every morning the Nyangi (doctor) from each Camp goes from cell to cell to discover what happened during the night. To every visit the gangs send a witness (a *getuie*) to make certain that no inmate reports on gang activity to the visitors. Although the witness himself has no visitor he will tell the warder on duty that he is a *getuie* and the warders comply because it is easier, and the consequences, if they refuse to allow the gangs to follow procedure, could be very unpleasant indeed.

Any gang member who wishes to see a doctor or a social worker or even his lawyer must get permission from the Glas and Draad in his Camp.

It's said that the only legitimate way to leave the gang, and survive with body and mind intact, is to become converted, to become an adherent of another religion.

Old-time gangsters indulge themselves by reminiscing how stringently the rules were applied in *the good old days* when a new recruit was not allowed a visit from his family and even leaving his cell during his training period was absolutely forbidden. They boast about how tough they were, when violence against warders was the order of the day and men were beaten and thrown into solitary confinement on a whim. They bemoan the changes that indicate, to them, a weakening of the gang structure. But they are misreading the signs. There is no need at present for the violence that existed in the prisons during the *apartheid* era. The gangs have far more freedom to carry out their activities without any interference. They no longer need to fight the staff. Excessive violence at present could sound The Number's death knell in the prisons.

The Number Gangs have endured over many generations because they are experts at successfully managing the lives of prisoners from inside the prison system itself. When external demands force them to adjust, they tend to respond in a manner that will neither compromise their rigid structures and lines of communication nor threaten the boundaries that separate the 28s from the 26s and 27s, boundaries that must be respected to maintain equilibrium within The Number and prevent the system from collapsing into anarchy and chaos.

There is nothing haphazard or spontaneous – nothing left to chance, no space for deviation – in the world of The Number. The members of the Number Gangs are rigidly organised. They are the most disciplined of soldiers. They are the most indoctrinated cult members anyone could ever encounter. They have a strong sense of loyalty to the gang and fear, of unspecified repercussions, plays a major role in ensuring that devotion to The Number remains paramount above all other issues including that of personal safety. There is no prisoner who has not seen the consequences for those who have spoken out against gang activity or for those who have broken gang rules or disobeyed orders. There is no place to hide in prison. The gang will reach you no matter where the authorities transfer complainants and their witnesses. As a result it is almost impossible for men, whose human rights and dignity have been infringed upon, to lay complaints against Number Gang members and succeed.

Because of the lack of vision in the Department of Correctional Services there has never been an opportunity to give any other system a chance. What is needed are single cells, compulsory work and study programmes for every inmate, drug-free units and conjugal visits. These changes would weaken the power of The Number. But it's never going to happen.

Chapter Three

 **Historicity**

*a brief summary of the historic milestones that impacted on the life
and ambitions of Mzozephi Mathebula*

the nguni in 1600

Kwazulu Natal is a mostly sub-tropical coastal region on the east coast of
Africa. It's situated below the equator and bordered by the foothills of the
great, icy Drakensberg Mountains on one side and the warm Indian Ocean
on the other.

The area where Mzozephi was born was settled by the 1600s. It was
home to the Zulu-Xhosa-Swazi-Pondo people, the Nguni, who share a
related language as well as culture. For generations Mzozephi's people had
lived, died and honoured their ancestors and practised their traditions in
their kraals, collections of beehive shaped huts, on the slopes of the hills of
the Zulu. The Zulu fought in direct combat, not at a distance with
gunpowder and cannon, they honed their skills in hand-to-hand combat and
were experts at wielding spear, knobkierie and shield.

1600 to the trek

The Southern tip of Africa was settled, also in the 1600s, by invaders from
Holland who set up a half-way house in support of the Dutch ships on their
way to barter for commodities in the East. The settlement at the Cape was
controlled by the Dutch East India Company, a money-hungry, profit-
engendering private organisation. When a century and a bit later the affairs
of Europe impinged upon the settlement and it looked as if the French, an
unfriendly power, might take control of the Cape, the British stepped in.

After the defeat of Napoleon in 1815 and the end of the Napoleonic Wars
some money changed hands and the British stayed put. The local Dutch-
Afrikaner population were not impressed. In the early half of the eighteen-
hundreds a significant number of them left the Cape Colony. They decided
to trek north, taking with them their ox-wagons, guns, livestock,
possessions, women, slaves and religion. They sought independence and

personal freedom in the interior of the Dark Continent. Inevitably they encountered the Nguni tribes of Africa. To their horror and disgust these black men considered themselves to be the rulers of the hinterland. When these Voortrekkers infiltrated Zululand in the 1830s there was conflict and in 1838 Dingaan, the Zulu king – successor to the magnificent and terrifying Shaka who had united the Zulu into a single nation prior to his death – killed the trekker leader, Piet Retief.

beyond trekking

The Black-White conflict was to continue for another fifty years during which period the British, great world colonisers and empire builders, arrived to commandeer the little port of Durban and to disenfranchise both trekker and Zulu with one hand while defeating the Xhosa nation, living on the borders of the Cape, with the other.

In accomplishing the latter they were ably assisted in 1856 by the false prophetess Nonqawuse, the maiden who advised the Xhosa nation to slaughter all their cattle, promising that *the ancestral spirits would drive the whites into the sea and new herds would replace the dead animals.*

From the Xhosa nation's compliance one can tell to what levels of despair and desperation they had been reduced in the face of the guns and men from Europe. It was little short of total national suicide.

Of course the British were most saddened by the repercussions and the suffering. They took immediate advantage. Starving black Africans were reduced to servant status in white households. It was whispered: "The Xhosa, poor things, have only themselves to blame." The wars, which had gone on for some thirty-five years were over. White-benevolence was now the name of the game.

One of the men involved in the negotiations with the tribes was Sir George Grey (1812-1898) Governor of the Cape (from 1854), who was no lover of the Xhosa. We hear more of him later when we interpret the bizarre history of the 26 Gang.

british diplomacy

In 1867 – at the time of the birth of Mzozephi in the Land of the Zulu (later to be named the Province of Natal and today known as Kwazulu Natal) – the Cape was a British Colony and the independent Boer Republics of the Transvaal and the Orange Free State, created by the Voortrekkers via bribery, war and the expropriation of land, were in their prime.

In December 1878 – when Mzozephi was about twelve years old – the British presented the Zulu nation, now under the leadership of King Cetshwayo, with a series of demands directed against Zulu independence. More Zulu-Brit wars followed and a defeated Cetshwayo was imprisoned in the Castle in Cape Town.

In 1886 – with gold having been discovered – Southern Africa was an Aladdin's cave.

In 1887 – when Mzozephi was almost twenty and on the point of leaving home to take on the persona of Jan Note – Zululand was declared British territory. The Xhosa nation was already finished as a force to be reckoned with and now the Zulu nation was to be broken up into insignificant, impoverished, separate clans, nullifying all that King Shaka had achieved. With their impeccable timing the British had created a never-ending supply of cheap black labour to work those gold mines. God had to be on their side.

In 1897 – when Mzozephi, now known to his men as Nongoloza, was a man of thirty, leader of a pack of brigands and heading towards his first prison sentence – Zululand was annexed to Natal. All that was left for the Brits to do was to vanquish the recalcitrant Afrikaner. This they accomplished, though not as easily as predicted, by winning the Anglo-Boer War in 1902.

Chapter Four

Bad Boy to Brigand

details of the life of Mzozephi as he prepares for a collision course with the authorities and adopts the pseudonym of Jan Note

naughty mzozephi

Mzozephi was reared according to the traditions of his culture. He possessed as his birthright, as do all men of his race, the Zulu's natural pride and dignity. It was drilled into him: *the Zulu nation fought the British and Afrikaner bravely and ferociously, defeating them and outmanoeuvring them on many occasions.* But, despite this, with the onset of adulthood, he was just another black man in a disempowered nation ruled by those with white skins who spoke unmelodic languages called English and Afrikaans.

Mzozephi, like many young men, had dreams and aspirations, but there is some indication – based on his sexual history – that Mzozephi's activities with the young maidens of his tribe went a little further than the consensual *between the thighs sex* that was permitted courting Zulu couples. It became expedient, imperative even, for him to make the first of his quick exits before he ended up on a collision course with the village elders.

jan note the farm-boy

Mzozephi took the more westernised name of Jan Note, so much easier for the white man's tongue to pronounce, and joined his extended family working for a farmer in the Harrismith district.

His career as a farm labourer was blighted and his reputation was again called into question, when his master's horse vanished.

There is no proof that Jan Note, still known as Mzozephi to his family, ever stole that horse, but he was far too intelligent to have offered his services to an unjust employer who diddled his labourers out of their earnings and, as subsequent actions indicate, he *liked to pull a fast one* especially when he thought he could get away with it.

When he was called upon to make restitution, by working for two years without payment, Mzozephi bolted and it is interesting to note that his 'brother' did not appear to believe him to be innocent and gave him no support or encouragement.

Mzozephi, or Jan Note as he was now called, headed north. He was, however, not in the fortunate position of Dick Whittington who set out with nothing and became Lord Mayor of London. As a child of a vanquished nation Mzozephi Mathebula's real-life choices were limited. His only chance of survival far from his family, was to learn the outsiders' tongue and once again to place himself at their disposal as a source of labour — poorly paid, under valued, little understood.

Living under white domination, no matter what his age or marital status, he could only aspire to becoming a farm-boy, garden-boy, house-boy or mine-boy. In the land of his birth, because he was black, he could never be a man.

jan note the house-boy

After the horse-debacle Mzozephi was employed as a houseboy by four white men in Turfontein, criminals and robbers, who lived beneath a hill close to the railway station. Their modus operandi was to don stolen police attire and use their false authority to stop, search and rob the gullible.

Curious as to their methods Mzozephi began his criminal apprenticeship and honed his entrepreneurial skills under two of these crooks — a Mr Tyson and a Mr McDonald.

Yet again he departed with no explanation. He was convinced he could work as well as they did — but with better results.

Regarding the 'lost' horse — much later in life Mzozephi declared he saved up three pounds to pay for the animal, but his 'brother' (putting in a fortuitous appearance) disappointed him and refused to act as go-between.

bad-boy mzozephi

Whether he was ever employed as a mine boy is not known, although he certainly gained knowledge of the mines. What is undisputed historical fact, taken from early prison records, is that, by the time he was in his mid-twenties Mzozephi had become, not a farm-boy, or house-boy or mine-boy, he had became a bad boy — a bandit. He'd found his niche at last.

Before 1900, before the outbreak of the Boer War between the British and the Transvaal Republic, Mzozephi was a committed career criminal and an outlaw, working with a band of brigands under the leadership of Nohlopa in the caves south of Johannesburg at a place called Shabulawawa in the hills of Klipriversberg.

Chapter Five

Nongoloza

the banishing of Jan Note, the vanishing of Mzozephi Mathebula and the creation of Nongoloza, risk taker and rebel, whose new alias identifies him as The Elevated One or The Rule Giver

leader of men

Joining the brigands was a revelation. At last Mzozephi was in the company of men – Zulu, Xhosa and Pondo – with similar cultural backgrounds, thoughts and aspirations.

He had come home!

When Nohlopa, the leader of the group of brigands, was arrested and converted to Christianity, Mzozephi made his move.

His was a magnetic personality and he was an opportunist. He might have been similar to his companions, but intuition informed him that he was vastly superior intellectually and he knew he had a great vision for the future. He adopted yet another pseudonym and, as Nongoloza, he took over leadership of a group that numbered over two-hundred men.

Nongoloza was not a man to suffer from self-doubt. He threw himself into creating his empire. He inspired complete loyalty in those who followed him and was in a position to put his personal imprint on his group of men. He was also an inspiring speaker and spellbinding storyteller around the campfires at night, his eyes staring right through his men and plumbing their souls to the very depths. Combining these qualities with his manipulative attributes, strong survival instinct and the ability to take risks, meant that he quickly developed into a force to be reckoned with. He amalgamated aspects of both the European and Zulu nations to build a secret society that would fight on his behalf throughout his lifetime and for almost a century after his death.

Before long his men were mesmerised and he was greeted with "Bayete!" the salute reserved for Zulus of the Royal House.

One cannot help being awed by his charisma, terrified by his sheer guts. His life-story would make wonderful cinema. It's surprising no one has attempted it. One stands astonished, admiring his achievements, even against any better judgement.

The following names appear in the history of The Number:

Nongoloza: *born **Mzozephi Mathebula**, alias **Jan Note**; referred to as **Nkosi Nkulu** and **Madala One** (an elder/chieftain) in prison. He was the founder of the Number Gangs and a Zulu. He heads the Camp of 28. Nongoloza means Elevated One and Giver of Rules. His rules were written on a white stone. He was born in 1867 and died in 1948. His mother is said to have been **Nompompo** (The Tap) and she was the wife of **Headman Numisimani**.*

Ngilikityane: *pronounced Kilikijan in the Western Cape; the name Ngilikityane means 'the man who moved, bumped or knocked the small stone'! This implies that he questioned the laws of Nongoloza pertaining to sodomy. He broke away to head the Camp of 27. He is known in prison as **Ntolombom** (Arrow of Life/Blood or The Protector) and also called **Makhwezi** or Shooting Star. He may have been the Xhosa man Jim Tanana who was called the Giant with the Squint Eyes and Big Head (Ntlokonkhulu).*

Grey: *the rather mysterious and controversial head of the Camp of 26.*

Pawule Mambazo: *is an imaginary figure from Pondoland. When Nongoloza developed his mythical history for the bandits he told the story from the viewpoint of a young man. The Camps of 26 and 27 know this character by the name of Pawule and the Camp of 28 call him **Ngulugudu** (a corruption of Nkhulunkhulu or Great One). Both names mean 'a person who is marked' or 'singled out' or has 'special attributes'. This character sits on the pure white stone and he sends Nongoloza and Ngilikityane on a mission. They must kill the bull **Rooiland** belonging to the farmer **Rabie**. The Afrikaans inmates call this character Po, the English speakers Paul. There are hints of St Paul and the revelation on the Damascus Road.*

Magubaan: *'ma' indicates female; he was Nongoloza's lover. It is not known if he was a real or symbolic figure; in the gang he is also Goliath.*

*Clearly the white man was no stranger to the Zulu, his reputation travelled ahead of him. Interspersed in the gang-history are also references to **the frans** (innocent new prisoner), **Hollander** (the aggressive 27s) and **geBritish** - an armed man.*

organiser and administrator

With the leadership responsibilities of his new position on his shoulders Nongoloza formed his men into a regiment that would have done Shaka Zulu proud. As with Shaka's impis, the company of women was forbidden to his group of robbers. There would be nothing to distract them from their purpose. He insisted: *There will be no women in this nation – other than those we create.* Nor had he qualms about borrowing skills from the British, the conquerors. They had defeated the Zulu and just about everyone else they had come into contact with. They had developed a system that worked well. If he was going to compete with them then he would follow suit.

He created a tight structure for his men based, not on Zulu traditions, but on the European legal and military hierarchy with clear lines of communication and certain punishment for those who disobeyed or absconded. It is this self-same structure that prison Number Gangs countrywide rely on in the New Millennium.

Like any other complement of soldiers his men were expected to keep fit and to drill regularly. To help them forget their families they took an oath of brotherhood. He expected his men to learn everything off-by-heart. This was quite acceptable to them. Africa has an exciting oral tradition. Although Nongoloza himself had learned to read and had studied the bible, absorbing the high-flown rhetoric of the prophets of the Old Testament, his men preferred to trust their memories. They had been trained in this method since early childhood.

He renamed the group *Umkosi wa Ntaba* (The Regiment of the Hills), and he moved them to a superior location. By the turn of the 19th Century his men were inhabiting abandoned, disused mine shafts outside Johannesburg. They got really lucky during the Boer War years (1899-1902) when all the mineworkers were sent home. The authorities had more pressing matters to deal with and Nongoloza had free rein hijacking groups of migrant labourers.

The brigands thrived. His men were impressed.

Years later, in prison, Nongoloza wrote (quoted in Haysom from the Dept. of Justice Annual Report 1912) wistfully and perhaps regretting – like all prisoners – the loss of his freedom and the fact that he had sacrificed a normal family life for one of crime: *The system I introduced was as follows: I myself was the Inkosi Nkulu or king. Then I had an Induna Inkulu styled Lord and equivalent to the Governor-General. Then I had another Lord who was looked upon as Father of us all and styled*

Nonsala. Then I had my government who were known to us by numbers, number one to four. I also had my fighting general on the model of the Boer Vecht generaal. The administration of justice was confided to a judge for serious cases and a landdrost for petty cases. The medical side was entrusted to a chief doctor or inyanga. Further I had colonels, captains, sergeant majors and sergeants in charge of the rank and file the Amasoja or Shosi, the soldiers.

It must have been hard for him to accept that it had come to this, four walls and capitulation, reduced to pleasing his captors so that he could achieve an early release.

philosopher

Being the opportunist that he was, Nongoloza directed his men to rob, not wealthy whites, but their own black brethren. He stole from the poorest of the poor and from the most oppressed. The prison Number Gangs in the New Millennium use the same tactics. They do not challenge the *sterkbene*, the strong. Although Nongoloza himself had been a migrant worker his Regiment of the Hills targeted black miners returning to their kraals with their pay packets tucked into their belts.

There was no lack of prey. Some 3000 men went on foot to the goldfields each month and statistics, provided by van Onselen the historian, tell us that there were about 1000 black men on the move between Johannesburg and Kimberley at any one time.

Under Nongoloza the brigands also adopted the trick of impersonating officials (*abathelisa*) and it was one easy step from this to invisible ranks and uniforms once the gang members went to jail.

When confronted with the fact that he was robbing his black brothers he listened to the muted murmurs and probably replied with a reasoning his men could not gainsay: *'Surely it is correct to prey on anyone who is aiding and abetting the white men to become wealthier, more powerful?'*

He was astute. He motivated his men with stories of white brutality towards blacks: *'Blacks are dying working for white men.'* He most likely told appalling stories of terrible conditions in the mines — of exploitation of the black man, of the suffering of the sick and injured: *'We must do all in our power to stop men from going to the mines and the best way to accomplish this is to rob the miners of their goods and cash on their return to their kraals. We make them suffer so that they can see there really is no dignity in selling themselves into slavery to help the white man get rich quick. Are they really our brothers? Whose side are they on? It is you, my soldiers, the Regiment of the Hills, who remain true to our roots. We are robbing sell-outs.'*

Before anyone refuted his argument he would add with an engaging grin: *'Besides, these men can always go back and work again and earn more money.'*

He'd figured it out, that it was okay; it was in the black nation's interests and in their own interests. In this way he rid them of their scruples.

This was typical of the inverted logic he employed. One encounters it again in his interpretation of the Christian Bible. Of course, some of the recently robbed would have stayed with the band of brigands thereby increasing Nongoloza's numbers. And this benefit was obvious to all. He lured miners to his side much as the present-day gangs in prison entice new members into their ranks.

From an objective perspective Nongoloza's idea of restorative justice was based on a wicked proposition, although he was convinced, and managed to convince his Regiment of the Hills, that what they were doing was indeed right and any losses incurred by their victims were well deserved. He manipulated his men, as he was to manipulate the prison warders when arrested. When doubts were expressed he knew he had the gift of the gab and could sweep away any misgivings, questions and fears in an instant.

Nongoloza was a most persuasive man.

mythmaker extraordinaire

The Zulu name Nongoloza means more than leader, it refers to *an elevated person, one who gives out or hands down the laws.* It's naïve to assume that Mzozephi was just drunk on power. To claim he had delusions of grandeur is far too simplistic an explanation for what subsequently occurred. Westerners know and understand little of the role and influence of the ancestors in African belief systems. In the absence of his family and especially after what he and his nation had endured, it is not too far-fetched to believe that Mzozephi was inspired and guided by the presence of those who had gone ahead of him, the ancestors who visited him in his dreams.

Whether or not the ancestors suggested the name of Nongoloza is a moot point. But certainly, it was all coming together to make perfect sense — in Mzozephi's head.

He re-organised history — creating his *Makhulu Book* (Big Book) that, with its *slasluka* (verses), repetition and imagery, resembles the bible. He had sufficient influence to apply his own time-frame, incorporating dates of his own choosing into the story of The Number, inventing an oral history rich in universal mythological symbols and biblical allusions.

He was in love with the power and the sound of words and particularly with the cadence, the tonal inflexions, of the Old Testament. He used a similar style – incorporating symbols and metaphors – when he developed his magical myth. Captivated by the language and stories of the bible, reared within an oral tradition in which fact and fantasy blur, his *Makhulu Book* still forms the basis of the Number Gangs' belief system.

When Mzozephi made the decision to become Nongoloza, to permanently assume a negative identity, South Africa probably lost one of the most forward thinking men this country ever birthed. He was a man of energy, of ideas. He was aggressive and seductive and able to inspire his followers with devotion and enthusiasm. He had powers similar to those of any modern influential political figure or cunning millennium business-magnate. What an asset he would have been to his people if he had lived in different socio-political times.

The man Mzozephi Mathebula, the originator of the Prison Number Gangs, existed in the world outside prison, that *other* world, the *umzakwaan*. We have a birth date and the names of his so-called parents. The prison authorities documented Mzozephi's milestones and he was interviewed in depth before he left prison. But, whether out of anger or shame over his birth-circumstances and given name – a name that applied abandonment by his natural parents – he covered the tracks of Mzozephi well. Neither the name *Jan Note* nor *Mzozephi Mathebula* is known to prison gangsters. They refuse to believe in their existence, relying instead on proven oral tradition. They are suspicious of anything that a warder, most likely a white man, committed to paper a hundred years ago.

From Mzozephi's personal viewpoint, possibly that was what the running, the crime at an early age, the adoption of pseudonyms, was all about — furious and confounded by his lack of knowledge regarding his own birth he created a negative identity of his own choosing.

Chapter Six

The Ninevites

What's in a name? From Nemesis to Nahum — from Ninevites to those Number Gangs

nemesis

Once the authorities - post Boer War - had come to grips with details for a settlement, they turned their attentions to the goings-on of Nongoloza. He was not going to be able to continue with impunity. After all, nothing should impede the flow of returning miners to and from their places of work. They could hardly run the mines without black labour.

Once large numbers of brigands and their captains were arrested the old appellation *Regiment of the Hills* fell away, they had lost the freedom of the outdoors. However, the laws they lived by were still being adhered to in the jails — living amicably without Nongoloza's rules proved impossible. They depended upon them to regulate group behaviour in an all-male environment, one in which they were subjected to much deprivation. In the prisons Nongoloza's men grew in strength and recruited new members. By the time the prison authorities cottoned-on to the fact that an unseen presence was running the prison system, Nongoloza had changed his gang's name from *The Regiment of the Hills* to *The Ninevites*.

The Book of Nahum from the Old Testament is described as an oracle concerning Nineveh and is based on a vision of Nahum the Elkoshite. Nahum is one of the least coherent, but most verbally flamboyant, visionaries of the Old Testament and particularly difficult to interpret in the St James Version of The Bible — which is the one that Nongoloza, who read and spoke English, most likely possessed.

An oracle is a place where deities are consulted for advice or prophecy through the medium of a priest. In African traditional beliefs the sangoma (nyanga or iqira) would retire to a cave where members of the tribe could apply for a consultation. Nongoloza had always been fascinated by the Bible, particularly the vibrant, wildly exhortative voices of the prophets, which both incite and admonish. But his personal attraction to the Book of Nahum was logical in view of his lifestyle — *thy crowned are as the*

41

locusts, and thy captains as the great grasshoppers, which camp in the hedges in the cold of day, but when the sun ariseth they flee away, and their place is not known where they are.

📖

Nongoloza disclosed to his jailers: *"I read of the burden of Nineveh. The book of the vision of Nahum the Elkoshite in the book of Nahum in the bible about the state of Nineveh which rebelled against the lord and I selected this name (Ninevites) for my gang as rebels against the Government's laws."*

Nongoloza was on a mission. Always a deep thinker, there were as many layers to his personality as there were strings to his bow. He understood that the Ninevites were evil. He identified totally with their dissolute and disobedient natures because, as he saw it, their argument against God was a righteous one, as honourable as his own stance against an alien white government.

Having chosen the negative identity, he joined battle with the forces of evil against good. Nongoloza's purpose was to challenge God himself!

ninevites

It is quite clear in the Book of Nahum that God means business: *Woe to Nineveh, woe to the city of blood, full of lies, full of plunder, never without victims.*

God — angry, powerful and vengeful, wished to punish the Ninevites. In a similar manner, the government, having subjugated Nongoloza's people, wished to destroy Nongoloza.

We read in the New International Version of The Holy Bible: *From you Oh Nineveh has one come forth who plots evil against the lord and counsels wickedness...you will have no descendants...you are vile...* It seems that the identification with the rebellious and corrupt Ninevites and their wicked counsellor was immediate, as was the allusion to no descendants — apt if they were having same-sex relationships.

While Nahum raged – *God is jealous and the lord revengeth and is furious* – Nongoloza remained cool, simultaneously identifying himself with God victorious, but also as the evil that God wished to annihilate. He was the oppressed and oppressor ...*take ye the spoil of silver, take ye the spoil of gold.* Subversive activities were his speciality. As The Ninevites they would win back some territory, any territory, for the black man. *The Lord is slow to anger, and great in power, and will not at all acquit the wicked: the Lord hath his way in the whirlwind and in the storm, and the clouds are the dust of his feet.*

It can hardly be coincidence that The Lord is the designated and invisible head of the Gang of 28.

Nongoloza allowed his hatred of the system to sanction the violence that he propagated against his own people. His legacy is grounded in a bitter resentment against a social, political and economic system that reduced him to the status of an inferior citizen for his entire life.

Following his guidelines a repetitive self-destructive pattern is re-enacted, as generation after generation of prisoners follow gang instructions that prevent them from working in any independent or meaningful manner within the limited rehabilitation programmes that the prisons introduce. Every act and every thought is controlled by and belongs to Nongoloza and reflects his hatred of mainstream social values.

With democracy we do not see a lessening of gang control, but rather an intensifying of gang activity.

number

Haysom (basing his information on an unpublished private paper by van Onselen) tells us that by 1903 the gangs had spread to the foothills outside Pietermaritzburg. By 1906 the Ninevites operated in and out of prison and the gang was also known as *People of the Stone* and sometimes simply as *Nongoloza.*

In 1908 Nongoloza, now aged forty, was in Volksrust Prison (not his first experience of imprisonment) on the Natal-Transvaal border. After escaping and burgling the local magistrates court – stealing revolvers and rounds of ammunition, retreating to the Swaziland border, robbing and shooting with impunity en route, raiding the hotel dining-room in Barberton (where a splendid meal had been laid out for a civil reception) and shooting an African policeman – he was recaptured, transferred to Pretoria Central Prison and sentenced to life-imprisonment for attempted murder. He was issued with a uniform stamped IS – *indeterminate sentence* – on the back. A move the authorities had adopted to break the spirit of The Ninevites.

But even from prison he controlled his bandits and when inmates were released they were better organised and more capable than ever before. His management strategies had preceded him and he used the rickshaw boys in the station yards to keep gang members informed, much as criminals today use modern taxi ranks.

□

After the brutal stabbing to death in 1910 of Constable King, a white man, the authorities really sat up.

By 1912 they had put their systems in place.

The gangs were flushed out of the mineshafts along with their remaining leaders Xaba, Schoko, Nyabezi and a mysterious Xhosa speaking general named Jim Ntlokonkhulu (Big Head).

From 1912 the gang operated almost solely within the prisons and remained there for almost eighty years until, in the late 1980s and early 1990s, reports begin to appear in the press. The notorious prison gangs, now called the Number Gangs, were once again out in the open. On the outside, operating and recruiting members in the communities and (true to their roots) forming bonds with street gangs, their focus was on controlling a burgeoning drug market.

The use of the title The Number, as an accredited name for the prison gangs, was unknown until the gangs were defeated on the outside and operated only within the prisons, in fact, up until 1920 they were still referred to as The Ninevites and sometimes as People of the Stone – a reference to the stone on which their laws were inscribed and possibly an allusion to the Ten Commandments! Up until this day many members declare that The Number is not the right name, but they are unsure what they should be called. The Number is certainly not a name Nongoloza would have chosen for his gang of bandits. He was far too flamboyant. We know that it is a title that developed within the prison system and is a title definitely related to the salutes and that is was a title introduced after the inauguration of the 26 Gang.

The appellation 'The Number' is possibly a name that prisoners who were non-gang members bestowed on a system that excluded them.

And it just happened to stick!

What is clarified, however, in their mythology, is that the symbolic salutes of 28 (raised thumb, index and middle finger) and 27 (raised thumb and index finger) were used prior to the arrest of Nongoloza as a convenient and immediate way for men to indicate to which branch of the Ninevites they owed their allegiance. Because, before Nongoloza's arrest in 1908, a separate division was created, a division that was to become the Gang of 27, to cater for men who did not want to indulge in same-sex practices.

44

Palace revolution

It is almost certain that the revolution in Nongoloza's ranks happened after the Ninevites moved to the disused mineshafts outside Johannesburg, but prior to Nongoloza's arrest in 1908.

When the gang made a decision to relocate to the abandoned mineshafts they were not empty. Other criminal elements were already in residence. That some amalgamation occurred between the groups is apparent because a new general appeared on the scene — a tall, lean, austere Pondo with harsh features and an ascetic nature.

It was this man, Ngilikityane (pronounce each letter as in English but the *y* as the *ch* in church and the letter *a* as *ah*), usually mispronounced and wrongly spelled as Kilikijan (by those not conversant with isiXhosa), who was going to challenge, not Nongoloza's leadership, but his principles.

Ngilikityane was not his real name. It is an appropriately symbolic name that has a close association with the stories of Nongoloza. In isiXhosa the word *ilitye* – meaning stone – forms the stem of Ngilikityane's name. Ngilikityane was *the man who bumped against, nudged* or *moved* Nongoloza's stone both physically and figuratively!

Unlike Nongoloza, who was a hedonist, Ngilikityane preferred celibacy to sexual relations with other men. This activity, according to Ngilikityane, debased the purity of the Ninevites. Soon the two generals, who had become blood brothers to cement a working relationship, would clash head-on. Ngilikityane intended to give Nongoloza's stone one mighty shove.

The gangs describe the confrontation between Nongoloza and Ngilikityane in biblical terminology and the impression it made on them indicates the reverence and awe in which their leader Nongoloza was held. Clearly the horror of the disagreement shook the Ninevites to their metaphorical core. The gang litany describes it as a terrifying upheaval, an earthquake, a cataclysmic event ...*the ground shook, the heavens and earth were rent asunder and the very stars fell from the firmaments*.

That the blood brothers had a serious disagreement over the issue of homosexual practices is not disputed and the fact that some men sided with Ngilikityane indicates that he had back-up. There may even have been a skirmish as there is some evidence that Nongoloza's catamite, Magubaan, sustained an injury to his head during the major battle at the crossroads. It is, however, far more likely that the exchange that took place was at a metaphorical crossroads and was one of debate and that this public debate set the tone for all future discourse.

📖

To this day, each time the gangs negotiate, their leaders – in the roles of Ngilikityane and Nongoloza – revisit *the crossroads* to engage, not with blows, but with words.

Being confronted by Ngilikityane was a new experience for Nongoloza. It was humiliating and disappointing, he and his blood brother had managed well together.

But, as always, Nongoloza kept his head.

He was known as a man of wisdom and a pragmatist. He would have viewed it as a suicide mission to weaken the Ninevites with violent internal conflict at a time when they were under increased pressure from the authorities. He'd given up too much to lose everything because of one man's naïve scruples. He would prefer to surrender some of his members rather than lose the whole. Not an easy decision, but one in the best interests of all. He led by example. He saw right into the hearts of his men. They knew him for a hard taskmaster. He exhorted his men to make personal sacrifices for the good of the movement and to put aside any thoughts of normal family life. He would now prove to those who owed him allegiance — he would not expect from his followers what he, himself, could not give.

In this way he would lose some of his adherents but those who remained would be more loyal, more committed, than ever before.

Throughout its history The Number has adjusted to circumstance as does any flourishing order that intends to survive.

A healthy sign, even for an evil system!

now we are eight

The gang split into two over the dispute regarding same-sex practices and some say this is where the number 28 and 27 came from as it alludes to the number of members in each division. Others claim there were fifteen and that 8 went with Nongoloza and 7 with Ngilikityane because the latter had to surrender the injured Magubaan and that *two* is a reference to the leaders.

The 26 Gang, however, have a magical, cosmological interpretation of how the 27 Gang got its name: "You see, when Nongoloza and Ngilikityane fought and Ngilikityane stood up to his knees in a river of blood, eight stars fell from the sky and the eighth star hit Magubaan on the head when it fell to earth, so there were only seven stars left. That's how the Number Seven happened."

And the 28s concur (up to a point) because, in prison, the inmate who plays the role of Magubaan still wears the bloodied imprint of that falling star upon his forehead.

What both gangs are very clear on is that Magubaan accompanied Nongoloza. Once again the incorporation of metaphorical names gives us no doubt as to the role of this youngster — *Ngubane* is a clan name in Zulu and the prefix *ama* indicates the female side of the clan. Later on Magubaan (also referred to in Afrikaans as the *aanhitser* or kindler of physical desire) reappears in the hierarchy of the 28 Gang. To indicate how powerful and important Magubaan's sexual role is in the maintenance of the gang they have renamed him Goliath (or Golia) — after the naughty giant who lost against the little good guy and ended up with a seriously wounded head.

Yet another example of Nongoloza's fascination with the negative identity!

now we are seven

Gang legend tells us that the two groups moved off in different directions to rob, murder and plunder across two provinces. Nongoloza, with twenty-eight men, proceeded initially in the direction of Delagoa Bay and Ngilikityane, with his group of twenty-seven, moved in the direction of Springs.

The decision to march was probably not only to do with the rift but also the increased risk of frequenting an area that the state was targeting.

This was not the end of the relationship between Nongoloza and Ngilikityane. They continued to co-operate when they encountered each other in prison. There is some evidence that there was fondness from Ngilikityane's side and that he idolised Nongoloza, was shocked when he discovered that Magubaan had seduced his idol.

now we are six

When Nongoloza and Ngilikityane met up in Pietermaritzburg Prison in Natal, some years later, they negotiated yet another agreement — to initiate men in a third arm of The Number. Between them Ngilikityane and Nongoloza created the Gang of 26.

This is not all hearsay. Prison records do indeed indicate that a man, known as Nkulu Zulu, received a prison sentence in Natal in 1903.

There is more than one version of how the 26 Gang came into being. And, naturally, each gang's version puts them in the pole position.

According to the simplified version six men helped Ngilikityane by supplying him with luxuries such as salt and tobacco while he lay in solitary confinement. As a reward they were permitted to form a separate branch of The Number, one that specialised in smuggling and theft.

The 28s' version describes how Nongoloza and Ngilikityane found six men crouched down over a white cloth on which lay a pile of coins. At first they thought to rob the six. Ngilikityane took their coins and shot one into the air, it fell on the ground and Nongoloza picked it up. Nongoloza wanted to wipe the six out, take their cash, use the coins as *spykers* or as buttons, but Ngilikityane persuaded him that these gamblers (men who could take a chance and win) would be of use to The Number in prison.

Another version tells us that when Nongoloza and Ngilikityane were in prison those doing light work (the females) helped Nongoloza, but Ngilikityane had no one to help him except the six men he had protected from the sexual predators in the 28 Bloodline.

Ngilikityane fought once more with Nongoloza, this time to protect the six. In return the six men smuggled commodities to Ngilikityane when he was sent *agter die berge* (into solitary confinement) for fighting. Ngilikityane gave permission for the men to create the 26 Gang and, as a result, the 27s always fight on behalf of the Gang of 26.

📖

According to a 26 gangster interviewed: "The Number 26 and 27 form one camp, much as the male and female lines of the 28 gang form one camp. And it happened like this. Because there was no ground (ground being a metaphorical word for turf – as in gangster turf) left in the prison for the six gamblers to form another camp, Ngilikityane and Nongoloza discussed the issue and Ngilikityane *het sy grond gesny* (gave a piece of his camp) so that there would always be place for the six men and that settled the matter." According to the 28s, Ngilikityane had to obtain the agreement of Nongoloza (or possibly his representative) before this third branch was brought into being and between them they decided that 26 would be the last Number created. When Nongoloza, wary and exploring his situation, asked Ngilikityane what the latter would do if the six turned against him, an oath was sworn. In return for allowing the six men to exist securely in prison (alongside the 27s and 28s) Ngilikityane promised always to stand between the six and Nongoloza and to keep the peace between them, apparently also agreeing to turn against the six if they destabilized the system.

This last statement may be pure wish fulfilment on the part of the 28s, because apparently it's never happened — 27s fighting against their 26 brothers.

The 26 Gang and 28 Gang have fought many times, with the 27s coming out in full support of the 26 Gang on each occasion. To allow the 28 Gang to save face, however, when the gangs negotiate the 26 Gang agrees for the purposes of keeping the peace, as a courtesy, and a convention, and an aid to communication, that their representative is always, for the moment (*vir die minute*) Ngilikityane the 27. It is always the general with *bloed en vleis* (armed) from *Grey se kant as Holland* who comes to negotiate at the crossroads. When the 28 wants to approach the Camp of 26 he always calls for Ngilikityane and the 26 calls for Nongoloza.

Nongoloza was willing to make a concession for Ngilikityane because he knew that the six men would be a support to The Number as a whole — would help maintain the system. In prison one cannot rely on force alone to rob. The warders, if they are watching, can come down hard on those who are too overtly aggressive. But men who had special skills, confidence tricksters par excellence, would be able to obtain commodities for The Number, especially money and drugs, without using violence.

Members from the Camp of 26 are also expert in identifying, initiating and training newcomers to the prison who possess similar qualities.

The six gamblers have, to honour their memory, been issued with names linking them to gang mythology:

1. Hlathini – forest or bush means *in prison, but not in a gang*
2. Zuka – the *money* that they gambled with
3. Dhazine – (from Ngasini?) means *What do I know?*
4. Kwedini – a young man (a *frans*)
5. Mpumi – a *reward* or *benefit* from the word mpumelelo
6. Pastu – possibly *pastor* from Afrikaans or English

Note the tightly woven symbolism: *There is an innocent boy in the prison who possesses money, but he knows nothing. He brings/gets a reward.*

The use of symbolic names aids memory and recurring symbols make for a tight structure when telling a story. The role of *Pastu* remains to be explored, but this could be the old man known as Grey.

It is tempting to speculate as to why Ngilikityane, after working well with Nongoloza over a period of time, suddenly took umbrage at his sexual shenanigans. Ngilikityane was no sissy. He was respected and feared as a man of violence and blood.

Now gang gossip informs us that Ngilikityane had a young son from a white woman (or so it is said), a bookkeeper and criminal, involved in gang activities. It's claimed that this son was one of the original six of the 26 Gang, and those members who support the story identify Kwedini — the boy. If this information is accurate then it seems logical that Ngilikityane was unlikely to have favoured the sodomising of his own offspring. He had both strong moral and personal motives to object strenuously to the activities of Nongoloza.

Although it cannot be proved, it can be inferred that this bloodlink is also the reason why the original band of 26 were so keen to assist Ngilikityane when he was kept in solitary confinement.

the man in grey

There remains yet another mystery. Who exactly is the individual the 26 Gang respect as Grey when the 26s repeat the slogan *Volle Nommer Grey?*

Some say Grey was already in prison when Nongoloza and Ngilikityane were arrested; some that he was *in the mines when Po arrived* (like Madala One). Others have claimed he was just *one of the six* who happened to be wrapped in a grey prison blanket; they may even suggest that Grey was the son of Ngilikityane. It is a difficult issue, because the reality of the prison experience for Nongoloza and Ngilikityane is frequently confused with their mythological history.

Senior ranking officers claim: "There were six men gambling and when Nongoloza and Ngilikityane approached them one of the men stood up and said *I am Grey.* He was their spokesperson and he had greying hair."

That this man had greying hair indicates European blood, that he was old indicates he could not be Ngilikityane's son, Kwedini.

These issues have puzzled gang members over the years and they have engaged in much discussion. This has resulted in the creation of a totally new persona for the man called Grey, a persona totally unfamiliar to gang members who left prison in the 1980s!

It seems that, in a more recently created myth, the man previously known only as Grey has been upgraded by an imaginative, creative Nogidela (the teacher of the soldiers in the Camp of 26), with more knowledge of South African history than the average prisoner and a conviction that the name Grey, standing alone, did not carry enough clout.

Sir George Grey is now identified as the symbolic head of the 26 Gang. There is documentation on the man Nongoloza that even verifies his birth date. There is evidence that Ngilikityane existed, although his birth name is in doubt. But the 26s have given themselves a leader with a respectable family tree. Talk about one-upmanship!

While the figures heading the Camps of 28 and 27 are very African, in complete contrast, Sir George Grey, who is now claimed as the representative of the 26 Gang (I am sure his descendants will be thrilled), was a white man, a central figure in Native Affairs for the Cape Colony. But then the 26 Gang also have historical links to a Scotsman (in fact they were once named The Scotlanders) and a white woman. They have always boasted a more European orientation while the 28s have a much more proudly African flavour with members armed – not with guns – but with assegai and knobkerrie and waving oxtails and carrying entrails. There are three legged pots of blood to be stirred and the first page of *The Book of 28* relies on African sangoma traditions and a snuff-taking ritual.

If probed by the more sceptical, as to the origins of Grey, 26 gang members will turn deadly serious and explain that the original six were not just *ordinary* robbers.

They specialised!

Apparently the original six were *grave robbers* and being really enterprising had, in the process, set up what can only be described as an illegal, unregistered, non-governmental welfare organisation (in keeping with events within the new South African democracy). Posing as church elders the six are said to have collected money for a place of worship they claimed that they intended to build for poor people who were worshipping on street corners. (Maybe this is where *Pastu* comes in?) But it was a scam. They kept the money.

This was an occasion on which I could not refrain from intervening.

"Where exactly did all this happen?" I butted in.

I was flashed an immediate response, "In Greytown, naturally. But of course they didn't use the money to build a church, they kept the money themselves. And were caught."

It seemed to me he was far too glib. But my informant was determined to convince me: "It *is* Sir George Grey because his head is on the money."

51

"But he was such a racist, how can you almost deify this man?"

"Well," came the thoughtful response, "he robbed too."

Caught out, I was forced to concede: "I guess he did help the British rob the black nations of their country."

"When he died, you know, the six found *all* his loot buried with him in his grave. Sir George Grey's bible and everything."

Too bizarre by far for my liking. A dead man, a ghost, as their leader?

But it just so happens that the 26 Gang do have a white flag (originally the grave cloth), symbolic coinage (money dated 1836 with Sir George Grey's head embossed on one side, six oxen pulling a wagon and a driver on the reverse) and they tattoo a bible on their chests. (This confirmed by a 28, *nogal!* So the rumours spread.)

While Sir George's head may well have been stamped on a medal, it would not have been on the coins of the day. These would have borne the head of the reigning monarch. I could not help connecting these symbols to the Great Trek of the same period. And the money? Had the six actually found and squandered the buried Kruger Millions? I was almost tempted to suggest it but controlled myself.

An objective researcher is not supposed to tamper with material or exert undue influence.

Sir George Grey arrived in South Africa as part of the British Administration. He was High Commissioner in 1854 and, within Native Affairs, a politically central figure who played a role in trying to sort out the issues surrounding the epidemic of lung disease which killed Xhosa cattle and again, in 1856, the slaughter of Xhosa livestock after the false vision of the young prophetess, Nonqawuse. He was involved in Transkei and British Kaffraria and during the Kaffir Wars he negotiated between Moshoeshoe and the Orange Free State.

Ngilikityane was of Pondo/Xhosa extraction and would have had some knowledge of Sir George, but little reason to respect him or introduce him as a hero into the Camp of 26. Sir George was firmly behind a course of action that saw Xhosa Chiefs – who obstructed British policies – arrested, banished and imprisoned on Robben Island.

Chapter Seven

 **Witbene**

Nongoloza negotiates, manipulates, capitulates and still manages to come up trumps

nongoloza: the captive

By 1912 the Ninevites were operating in prisons across the Transvaal and Natal and by 1919 they were in Noordhoek Prison in the Cape and Nongoloza was still serving a life-sentence.

The authorities were desperate.

New inmates complained bitterly that there were two authorities in the jails. They looked for direction as to whether to follow the instructions of the warders or of Nongoloza. If they objected to the activities of The Number then retribution was brutal. Men reported that they were beaten and their teeth knocked out or extracted. The warders were powerless to intervene or protect them.

The majority of prison officials were paid bureaucrats with no vision. They had no inkling that the myths of Nongoloza, drawing as they do on universal symbols, had embedded themselves deep down in the psyche of his men. They believed, somewhat simplistically, that if they could get Nongoloza out of the prison system, they'd get their prisons back.

During the latter half of 1912, through a warder named Paskin, the prisons negotiated with Nongoloza, offering him early release and a job as a native constable if he would just disclose exactly how his organisation operated. (Paskin was unaware that early in 1912 the devious Nongoloza, then in Pretoria Central, had already sent out a message to his men telling them that he wanted things kept quiet *for a while* as he was endeavouring to get his sentence reduced.) The authorities bribed him. They offered a lighter, shorter sentence, but he had to deny any gang involvement.

He capitulated. He was in his mid-forties and growing weary. Graciously he accepted their offer.

Or did he?

Firstly, his life work was accomplished. He could resign with pride. Secondly, he had outwitted the government and taken back a significant piece of territory for his nation. Thirdly, on a more mundane and mercenary level, the job of a native constable offered many opportunities for taking bribes. Fourthly, if a powerful governmental department was coming to him, cap in hand, the battle honours were his and his alone.

Nongoloza had set in motion a raging torrent. There was nothing he could do to stop it. But this wisdom he did not share.

📖

In a statement to the Director of Prisons – dated 27th December, 1912 – he explained: *The new law (indeterminate sentences and rules to isolate gang leaders) and the new prison administration have made me change my heart... I am quite prepared to go to Cinderella Prison or any other prison where the Ninevites say they get orders and to tell them that I give no orders even if it costs me my life. I would tell them that I am no longer king and have nothing to do with Nineveh.*

He made no mention of the execution of his close colleague, Jim Ntlokonkulu/Big Head (The Giant with the Crooked Eyes) who had been hung for murder in 1911.

📖

Nongoloza became a native warder at both Cinderella Prison and Durban Point Prison.

At the age of fifty (knowing exactly what the authorities wanted to hear) he spoke of his longing and love for cattle and the countryside and was retired to a kraal on a small farm in Swaziland — a reward from the government for being an obedient captive.

But, in the end, his need for dagga and alcohol got the better of him and he missed the adrenaline rush, the rape, pillage and plunder!

By the mid-1920s he was said to be back in the city, working as a warder at Weskoppies Mental Hospital and still nominally under the protection of the prison authorities who could not admit that their success story had fallen by the wayside.

When found guilty of the rape of a young woman they shipped Nongoloza off to work on a diamond mine in the Free State. After his release he took up casual work as a night watchman.

Like many prisoners, then and now, Nongoloza ended his life as a vagrant. Disowned by his relations, he died on the streets of Marabastad in Pretoria in 1948.

With no family to mourn over him or to claim his mortal remains, Nongoloza was given a pauper's burial. His bones lie in communal grave number 1438 in Native D Section of Pretoria's Rebecca Street Cemetery.

nongoloza: the anti-hero

Despite Nongoloza's capitulation it was too late. The Department of Prisons had lost the battle. The Number had already spread right across the country. The audacious Nongoloza was still running the show right under their noses.

Out-manoeuvred by a black man!

The prison authorities used the only tactic left to them if they wanted to save some face. They decided to ignore the presence of the Number Gangs and to pretend that they did no exist, had never existed.

nongoloza: the spirit

When Nongoloza died in 1948, at the age of 81 – sad, impotent, lonely, embittered, battle-weary – there was no one to honour his life or to mourn his death. No soul cared enough to plant a buffalo-thorn, the umphafa tree, in true Zulu tradition, on the old man's grave. This cruel omission proved a curse. There was no tree for his decaying body to feed. His spirit did not move slowly upwards through the branches. There was no calling home to his ancestors.

Deserted by Ngulugudu his lifelong guide, the dark spirit of Nongoloza has been left to wander for eternity in the prisons of this country. Probably the only genuine chance of countering his haunting presence is to locate his grave and plant that tree!

Part Two
the world inside

The book: absorbed in The Number the prison inmates live out their 'big moment in time' in a powerful and dangerous fantasy. All the instructions for how they should live their lives in The Number are provided in a big book, a Makhulu Book, for all the gangs. This book has never been written down, but exists only in their heads and is recited aloud when necessary.

The four walls: the prison is called the four walls and everything the gangs do within it is arranged according to whether they are 28s, 27s, 26s. The 28s will wait eight years before being initiated, the 26s six years (in real time frame they are referring to days). Meetings and initiation rituals are scheduled on the sixth, seventh or eighth day, depending on which gang is involved.

The mines: if the gangs recall any of their history prior to their existence within the prison system then it's their contact with the mines. There was not, during South Africa's early history, that much to choose from between prison and mine compound. In both the mines and prisons men were segregated from women and subject to much external control. After the Anglo-Boer War the British Regime, under Lord Milner, extended pass laws that restricted the movements of Africans and fingerprinted all mining employees to help identify workers who deserted. The state also supplied the mines with convict labour. The Ninevite influence spread and the words *mine* and *deep level* became synonymous with the prison and the gangs. The pass laws made it possible for many law abiding black men to work alongside convicts in the mines.

The symbols: when operating out of prison it is reported that the Ninevites were distinguished from other groups of bandits by their leg wrappings and headgear. With division in the gang came the need for new symbols that would differentiate one Ninevite from another. It seems likely that some prior agreement was reached, possibly some careful work-shopping between Nongoloza and Ngilikityane, as to the salutes that would be employed, the design of the flags and colours on the uniforms. And in prison, of course, the uniforms and flags are invisible.

Chapter Eight

A Potent Cocktail

words, symbols and colours that allow the gangs to distinguish one from another while they work towards a common cause

introduction

The complex codes of The Number specify how the gangs should approach each other so that formalities are observed; protocol states that the 26s rule by day and the 28s by night. Within the internal structure of each gang men are promoted depending on their performance or knowledge. When new recruits are to be initiated the gang concerned will formally notify their brothers in the other gangs of what is about to take place.

The week is organised so that meetings are planned in advance and held on the same day, strictly in accordance with gang tradition, at prisons across the country.

The three gangs are supposed to complement each other but battles occur over turf, membership, commodities (particularly drugs). The cell burnings and deaths in 2004-2005 at Pollsmoor Admission Centre were the result of inter-gang and intra-gang disputes.

language

The language the men use when conversing with each other probably developed as a response to the prison system and not as a form of rebellion. They merely wanted to communicate in secret. They speak a mix of English, Afrikaans and a corrupted version of Zulu or Xhosa. When reciting their oral history they will use their mother tongue as a base-line incorporating the coded Xhosa or Zulu words where necessary and Afrikaans patois, if Afrikaans is the home language. They employ many gang-related hand gestures whenever they speak, there are regular catch phrases and the noise of fists slapping against palms and fingers clicking introduces a nice musical accompaniment. The words employed are very emotive and play an important part in gang propaganda.

I was told: "You say it in your own language whether it is English or Afrikaans or Xhosa, it doesn't matter. You learn the book at night; even as you sleep you hear it in your head. You cannot make a mistake. All the same, many men do struggle to remember properly."

The 26s consider the language to be *fanigalore or shalambom* and claim it developed in the mine compounds. It is certainly not the version of fanigalore that miners speak, but it is a mix of languages. (And it is certainly not *funny galore* if the members do not learn their lessons properly!) The other word used to describe their speech is *salazisa*. When speaking in prison argot they refer to it as *sabela* or *the talk*. While *fanigalore* developed to aid communication between the miners as well as between miner and white boss, the prison language developed with the specific intention of aiding communication between initiated gang members from different cultural backgrounds while *totally excluding* the prison warders and those not initiated into the gangs.

📖

The man was eager to share: "I arrived by *stimela* (train) at Pollsmoor Maximum, without *botsing!*" He took pity on my confusion. "It means I was transferred to this prison but there was no fighting on my arrival." He continued to explain that his arrival, although he had senior rank, did not unsettle the equilibrium in the prison. If he'd been forced to fight to maintain his position there would be no possibility of asking for help for his predicament. "You get out of it yourself," he explained.

Naturally it was not a real train that brought him to Pollsmoor — but another convoluted metaphor. In this way, by using *just one single word* or *slogan,* he conveys a wealth of information to the initiated listener.

Incidentally: *stimela* (meaning a senior gang member who has recently been transferred to another prison) is a Zulu word and *botsing* is the Afrikaans word for a crash.

The 28s talk of *gazilams* (my blood) when referring to their brothers. In Zulu – *gazi* means blood and *lam* is the possessive pronoun – they have added an *s* for convenience. The plural in the Nguni languages being indicated by a prefix, never a suffix. The gangs will add an Afrikaans prefix to an English noun or adjective thereby turning it into a verb *hy was geBritish* translates as *he was armed.*

The men revel in learning the *sabela* and the accompanying litanies, which are practised ad infinitum until they know everything off-by-heart. They spend their lives debating and rehearsing the stories from The Big Book and demonstrating the power of their presentations instead of furthering their education.

📖

salutes, flags, coded colours

Each of the Number Gangs has its own salute. The 28 will salute with his thumb and first two digits; the 27 with the thumb and index finger; the 26 with the raised thumb. They will tell you *this is my sign, my flag, my gun, my pen.*

When standing at ease, waiting to be inspected, the man's hands are held behind his back, but always readied for his special salute.

The 28 may combine a salute with *Umsunukonyoko!* This is a specific reference to the mother's genitals. Although acceptable inside prison, this particularly vulgar word will cause a violent confrontation if used on a city street. When working with street children I noted that all they needed to say was *umsunu* or *jou ma se* and battle was joined.

📖

A detailed description of all the flags is given in the first page of The Book of 26, but the first page of the Book of 28 does not mention flags at all.

📖

He was such a horribly nice man full of energy and life and charm and he told me: "The colours on the flag of the 28 Gang are red and green and black and white, but certain colours are not visible." (This might appear confusing as of course the flag is *totally invisible*. But I nodded sagely!) "The flag of the 28 gang is green with a thick red line. The colour white is for the privates who never fight but do light work in prison (women's work), red is for the Gold Line, for the men who take blood, green is for the Silver Twos, the senior men in the Private Line. We never mention black – it is darkness for *witbene* (the dead) and not actually there on the flag."

The 28s' flag also includes a pictorial representation of a horn (out of which Nongoloza and Ngilikityane drank blood) and the profile of a lion's head to commemorate the traditional slaying of a lion when a Zulu man becomes a warrior. The 28s hotly deny that their flag symbolises the green veld and that the red line is the blood Nongoloza shed when he fought with Ngilikityane.

The 26 laughed: *"Daai wil hulle nie hoor nie!"*

The colours of the flag are again reflected in the 28s' symbolic building: white walls, red roof, green frames and a gold flagpole with their flag blowing in the wind. On the gate at the entrance to their camp they have inscribed the number 28, the eight in gold and the two in silver — gold indicates the male line and silver the female line. There is an almost obsessional need to ensure that everything ties in and fits neatly together.

61

Within the Camp of 28 the words Bloodline and Gold Line are interchangeable. For consistency in this text the word Gold Line is preferred when juxtaposed with Silver Line.

📖

The 27 flag is red as blood with crossed swords (blades pointing upwards) and a horn (or bugle) and seven six-point stars. It alludes, in pictorial form, to the battle between Nongoloza and his fighting general Ngilikityane and indirectly to the loss of Magubaan and the establishing of the 26 Gang (the six stars) in prison.

It would appear that these seven six-point stars are a fairly new addition to the flag. Could they have been introduced at the time South Africa got its own democratic flag in 1994?

📖

The flag of 26 is *pure* white to emphasise their ability to rob with a clear conscience. The symbol on their flag is money. A thin red line – their bloodline – indicates the need to involve themselves with blood when Ngilikityane is called upon to defend their camp. The thin red line is not visible in times of peace.

tattoos, terms, times

The Gang of 28 works at night and under cover of darkness. They have several signatures including the tattoo of a setting sun between naked buttocks. Because there is such a definite division in the Camp of 28 and their sub-culture, organised around sexual roles in prison, is of such critical importance, they have developed different ways of signalling to each other whether a man has entered the gang as a member of the Gold Line (male/aggressive) or as a non-dominant sexual partner in the Silver Line.

The words *Moliva Boy* (more than likely a corruption of *mooi lewe* - nice life - meaning an easy time as a female in the gang), tattooed on the upper left-shoulder, indicate the man entered the gang through the Silver Line. All allusions to the left-hand side indicate the Silver Line. The right-hand side indicates one is of the Gold or Bloodline and that the member has taken blood; this member will be referred to as a *man van bloed*. And if a man's heart is said to beat *three times* or *once* then he is of the Bloodline, but if it beats only *twice a year* it means he has been initiated as a private in the Silver Line.

The 28s have a range of terms, apart from the salute of *umsunukonyoko*, indicating sexual activity. Sex is sometimes referred to as poison (gif/*gal*) and the terms *giving water* or *not being allowed to drink water* are sexual

62

references; w*iping the sweat from the brow* is an indication that intercourse has taken place. If a 28 is described as drunk *he is drunk with lust;* if he is a *dronkie* he is drunk from taking blood. If they say a man cannot *skiet* it refers, not only to his being unable to take up a knife and stab to enter the Gold Line, but also to his being prohibited from engaging with another as the dominant sexual partner. He is a *wyfie* – the female in the 28 Gang. Although one must not use this term! I was warned: "*Wyfie?* No way! Do you want to start a war?" It's better to use the words *son, child, kind* or *boy*.

With sunrise the Gang of 26 has permission to do its work. And they always embrace the right-hand side to indicate that they shy away from same-sex practices. There are frequent references to *kroon* (money) in the 26 Gang. The 26 will refer to himself as *'n man van kroon*. Tattoos usually indicate a fixation with money. The man will display many dollar signs and coins on his body as well as a couple of fists clutching wads of cash and the motto: *I did it all for the love of money!* He may have a tattoo of a coin pierced by the point of a blade or a tattoo of an elaborate, stylised crown. Another favourite is an open book resembling a bible and usually tattooed on the chest with the number 26 on the open pages; or the date 1836 and the name Grey.

The 27 will display the crossed scimitars and the rising sun and the terms *vleis en bloed* are used when referring to a 27, *vleis* indicating either the possession of a firearm or weapon (traditionally a knife), or that the man is armed in some way.

Ngunyas – this is the Nguni word for stars and refers to a chief with rank. These stars (ranks) are tattooed like epaulettes on the shoulder. To complete the illusion of being westernised – despite their African origins – they live in *military camps* and *tents* — not kraals and beehive huts.

There are frequent allusions to *a stone* on which the laws of The Number were written. From 1904 up until 1920 the name People of the Stone was interchangeable with The Ninevites. There is the sacred skin (of the bull Rooiland) in the possession of Nongoloza and the 28s, which was wrapped around the stone. These symbols and the stories of the farmer Rabie, are taken from the early history of Nongoloza and Ngilikityane.

Symbolic place names include Twelve Points and the Four Points, a reference to the points of the compass, indicating that the parliaments (senior members) have been summoned to a *sitting*; and *die hekke* (gates) that the new recruit must enters to become a full gang member. The Crossroads is where the gangs meet to join in discussion over issues and recall the crossroads where Nongoloza and Ngilikityane had their famous dispute. Moliva River (into which the stone with the laws upon it rolled) is likely the Mooi River or *pretty river.*

The Sixes, who consider themselves to be the first *men in the mines* (in prison), bitterly resent any allusion to the 28s ever having worked in the mines. They grumble, "Most of the 28s say they were in the mines, but the 28s were never in the mines! Those 28s who speak of mines are *dom* (stupid). *Hy was nie in die myne nie.* But the real old 28, he knows where he comes from. Don't argue with him. *Hy kamandela vir jou* (catches you out)."

They will continue, seemingly without any logic: "The Sixes can give to the Sevens but never to an Eight. Only the Sixes can work with money. It's not allowed for an Eight." Just part of inter-gang myth — theoretically that's how it's supposed to work, that the mines equate with gold and money and the number 26. But in reality the 28s keep their own cash.

In actual fact the Ninevites operated in mine compounds long before the 26 Camp was envisaged. In 1912, the historian van Onselen recorded — *Nongoloza's men were often miners by day and robbers by night and the young boys on the mine compounds were sexually abused.*

the shotgun

During the gang ceremonies they practice *One Time Shotgun* — which gives the Inspector the power to do his work and opens the sessions at Twelve Points. The *Two Times Shotgun* allows the Nyanga (doctor) to proceed at initiation. The *Shotgun* ritual is also used to close meetings. Of course, no gun is fired. The men stand in a line, hands straight at their sides, readied to present arms. The right leg then stamps the salute, either once or twice, the body is angled forward and the right arm, bent at the elbow, is swiftly elevated to shoulder level and then returned to the side.

After this, reverting quickly to an African tradition, they will *down* — crouch on the ground (similar to a sangoma or witchdoctor crouched around his divining bones) in a circle with the thumbs resting on the ground if they are of the Camp of 26; two-fingers, if they belong to Camp 27 or with arms folded across the chest for the Camp of 28.

Now that's when they *sabela!*

Chapter Nine

From Eight until Late

the structure, roles, relationships and uniforms within the military and judicial hierarchy of the 28 Gang

introduction

The centuries pass but the Number Gangs remain at war with the authorities. They are unconsciously fulfilling their role as *The Ninevites* in opposition to God Almighty. As a result all three gangs have soldiers to carry out the duties of protecting the camps and senior ranks to issue instructions. There is a dual legal system: a lower court that disciplines minor breaches of regulations and a high court of justice that hands down death sentences and disciplines and punishes without benefit of an advocate. The Number Gangs continue to employ an efficient and sophisticated organisational structure based on a military and legal hierarchy and bolstered by their use of secret initiation ceremonies, a coded language, esoteric symbols and grim rituals.

the 28 gang

The 28 Gang is the one that has altered the most, recently closing off its Gold Line at awaiting-trial venues, such as Pollsmoor Prison, in the Western Cape. In theory the 28 Gang is supposed to fight for better prison conditions for all prisoners. In practise it is about sex and disputes over sex.

In Southern African society same-gender relationships are catered for and condoned in special religious circumstances (female sangomas may take an ancestral wife) or economic circumstance (where a widowed, infertile woman with possessions may take a wife to provide her with children born of another man). In times of war soldiers were permitted to take young boys into battle with them for sexual gratification. No officer wanted his man to desert, to go back and visit his wife in the kraal. And it is probable that Nongoloza, when he first set up his Regiment of the Hills, felt the same way.

My informant, with many *ngunyas* on his shoulders, was a high-ranking member of the 28 Gang, he was commenting on the civil war within the Camp of 28 in the Boland prisons in the 1980s: "*Die Sikhosi* (chiefs) *het uitgekom* because of the dispute between Gold and Silver Lines and there was within the 28 Gang great bloodshed as brother turned on brother. It developed over not building the *private line* so that the soldiers of the *blood line* did not have enough sexual partners to choose from and many rapes were the result."

To stop the war they murdered a Desperado, a member of another gang. After the murder *they ploughed and built The Number up again* — these ad hoc sacrifices are always necessary to cleanse the Number Gangs.

The result of the civil war in the 28 Gang is that all new recruits are now raped by ranking officers on entry into the gang — even the ones who will later claim Gold Line. Never again will there be too few *wyfies*. All men now begin their career as probationers, sexual service providers and enter *the cave* to be sodomised by senior gang members.

The gang has invented a cover-up. They claim they made a decision *to close* the Gold Line – the line in which men must stab to gain access – in prisons that accommodate awaiting-trial prisoners as 'these men may well be found not-guilty and released into the community half-way through their training.' If their reasoning is correct then why have the 26s not followed suit and why have all the gangs not decided to stop all gang recruitment until men have been sentenced?

No matter how they try to bamboozle or hoodwink, it must be understood that the main purpose of the 28 Gang in prison is to organise sex for the more aggressive males in the Gold Line.

Nongoloza himself told the authorities that homosexuality was a feature of the gang long before they moved into the prisons. Nongoloza was prepared to risk splitting the gang into two divisions for the sake of continuing his same-sex practices. The members of the gang are carefully schooled as to what to say if questioned about sexual activity in the Silver Line. They will explain that Silver Line members are chosen for their intellect and that the story of *wyfies* in the camp of 28 is just that, a lie invented by the 26s.

They shrug casually: "Oh, *wyfies*, that's just something the Sixes invent!"

In fact a sophisticated arrangement exists in the Camp of 28 that enables the senior gang members to obtain sexual satisfaction with a permanent, designated partner while men who come in as probationers (the lowest rank in the Silver Line) are forbidden the role of the dominant partner in a sexual relationship and are termed *wyfies* (an Afrikaans endearment: *little wives*).

The Silver Line (Amasilvers – *ama* being the plural in Zulu and Xhosa) as a term, was already in use in 1910 to honour a man called Joseph Silver who, in the 1890s, was one of Johannesburg's most notorious and successful pimps. But the senior gangsters are ignorant of this. They have their own version, which is part of the 28 history and which centres around Ngilikityane dropping the stone (with the laws written on it which confirm the acceptability of same-sex activity) into the Moliva River: "Magubaan went to swim in the river (to fetch the stone), he came out covered in drops shining in the sun like a fish, like a piece of silver, and that is where the name *silver line* comes from."

The 28s add that the stone hit a tree as it rolled down the embankment and that Ngilikityane took the bark of the tree on which only half the laws were imprinted and was satisfied with this, whereas Nongoloza got Magubaan to retrieve the stone and wrap it in the skin of an ox (Rooiland) and on this skin the full law permitting same-sex practices was imprinted.

Naturally, informants are eager to explain that the Gold or Bloodline can be re-opened if they *skoffel die grond met bloed*, plough the ground with blood. The gang would have to storm the entrance in an Admission Centre and stab the warders. Until the order is given to do this the blood rank is not *vasgebrand in die bomvana*, branded in their veins.

They have to stab, take blood to reactivate the line to be true *vleis en bloed* men of the Camp of 28. This closing of the Gold Line, even if only temporarily, is yet another example of accommodating to circumstances. The demilitarisation of the staff of the Department of Correctional Services, a more humane attitude towards inmates, plus the opening of the prisons to outside organisations, has generally seen a reduction in violence in the prison gangs. They can get what they want without fighting for it.

While it is easy to say that the Gold Line is fading into history, in a similar manner to the Camp of 27 (also categorised as *men of blood*), this assumption is brought into question when one considers that all three gangs combined in a revolt at Brandvlei Prison in 2008, a revolt that resulted in the stabbing of several warders.

The Brandvlei revolt occurred when prison authorities clamped down (too hard as far as The Number was concerned) on gang activities and drug smuggling.

The 28 Gang has three separate divisions:
1. The **Gold Line** (Blood Line/Red Line) – these are the males in the gang who enter by taking blood through the stabbing of a warder.
2. The **Silver Line** (Female Line/Private Line) – they supply (on demand) sexual favours to the Gold Line.
3. The **Third Division consists of the fighting soldiers of The Gold Line** – these are men who may not take part in sexual activities; fighting soldiers may have no contact at all with the females in the gang, also known as *wyfies*, they may not so much as accept an item from the hand of a *wyfie*.

The Gold Line /Division One
The Lord presides over the *high command* of the Military Wing of 28.

The Military Wing of the Gold/Blood Line
1. **The Judge** (Magielou-gielou also known as Judge Lantaba – from the Zulu word for mountain)
2. **The General** (Umsaza/Oom or Uncle Saza/Oemsasa) — *uncle* is a variant and may be a misrendering of the prefix *um* in Zulu/Xhosa which precedes many nouns and would sound, to a researcher speaking Afrikaans and with no knowledge of an African language, as if his informant were referring to *oom* or uncle.
3. **The Colonel** (Umfailand – no etymology identified; possibly connected to the fact that he keeps the skin (*skoemba*) of Rooiland the Ox on which the laws are inscribed); he also holds the post of the Ntshontsho (an interpreter who colluded with the police) the spy in the Camp of 28.
4. **The Wireless Operator** (Draad in Afrikaans/Ncancingolamoya in Zulu)
5. **The Lieutenant** (Jim Crow; also known as the Germiston after a railway junction in Transvaal) — Jim Crow refers to a segregationist; in this case it is **sexual segregation**; he decides whether the *wyfies* will go to senior officers in Division One or Division Two; similarly the Germiston gives the signal to change sexual tracks.

Number Threes or the Third Division of the Gold/Blood Line
There are four non-commissioned officers who preside over the fighting soldiers or *masjallou* (amasoja/shosi).
1. **Captain One**
2. **Captain Two**
3. **Sergeant One**
4. **Sergeant Two**

The Silver Line/Division One
The entire Silver Line is headed by **Nozala**: the **Parent Figure** who sits in the clouds. The *high-command* of the civil wing of the gang of 28 consists of posts held by males who were once *wyfies* but have risen in status.

The Civil Wing of Division One of the Silver Line
1. **The Governor General** (Mtshali/Blacksmith)
2. **The Doctor** (Nyanga/Nyangi)
3. **The Inspector** (Mafotsha/Die Glas/ Binoculars) he is also able to act as Die Glas in the Gold Line if there is a vacant post. He has the power to bestow (for a temporary period) a higher rank on an underling if there is a vacant post.
4. **The Clerk** (Mabalang / from the word *to write* in Zulu)
5. **The Magistrate** (Goba)
6. **The Under Magistrate** (Landdros/Public Prosecutor)

The Silver Line/Division Two
Below the Big Brass of the Silver Line are the probationers (privates/females) who are supervised (much like women in a harem) by:
1. **Goliath One/Golia**
2. **Goliath Two/Golia** (also called the Colonel's child)
3. **Silver/Masilver One**
4. **Silver/Masilver Two**

law and order in the camp of 28
Each section has a court to maintain order, ensure that the Code of 28 is adhered to and to proclaim sentences, hand down judgements and administer punishments. To differentiate between the courts they refer to points of the compass, points that indicate direction when one is lost or unsure of the right path.

The High Court of the 28 Gang handles major decisions such as battle procedures, policy, problems that affect the gang; this court swears in new recruits and tries cases and has the power to hand down the death sentence. The Judge is only present when the death sentence is recorded.

The Twelve Points decide on all serious judicial and other matters including declarations of war.

The Four Points deal with breaches by the Gold Line soldiers.

The Twelve Points

The Divisions Combine when the High Court sits. The six members (definitely not 12 members) consist of three officers from the Gold Line and three from the Silver Line.

1. Colonel (chairman) – Gold Line
2. General – Gold Line
3. Wireless Operator – Gold Line
4. Magistrate – Silver Line
5. Doctor – Silver Line
6. Clerk – Silver Line

The Four Points of the Gold Line

The Sergeants and Captains of the Number Threes head this court which deals with martial law and breaches of the code by the soldiers of the 28 Gang.

The Four Points of the Silver Line

Goliath One and Two and the Amasilvas (Amasilvers) One and Two handle minor cases in the Private Line. Goliath One is in the chair.

sexual practices in the camp of 28

The gang, while on one hand denying that sex takes place, reports, on the other hand, that the sexual contact is *between the thighs only* and is in keeping with Zulu courting practices. The rise in AIDs related deaths amongst prisoners indicates otherwise. This is not to say, however, that originally, when the gang had access to young boys – because adolescents were not separated from adults in prison and there were no labour laws to prevent young children from being employed in mine compounds – that they did not practice *between the thighs* sex. Under Nongoloza, men were not allowed to have full anal sex with their young boy-wives until they attained the rank of *ikhela,* a title given to Zulu men who had the chief's permission to marry.

The fact of the matter is that today it is penetrative sex and only the male is permitted to obtain pleasure in this manner. The applying of the juvenile justice system also means that young children are separated from men. The 28s have no choice but to assign the female role to another adult male.

The designated *wyfies* from the Silver Line are forbidden to penetrate. They are treated as women and given female tasks to perform. They are referred to as children (*kind* in Afrikaans) or wives (*little women* or *wyfies* in Afrikaans) or as seuns (sons); their sexual partner is referred to as their *babba* (father in Zulu).

The senior Gold Line ranks are expected to maintain a sexual relationship with junior ranks in the Second Division of the Silver Line while the soldiers in the Gold Line are (in theory) not allowed any contact with the *wyfies*.

Senior Ranks in the Gold Line and their Sexual Partners
Division One in the Gold Line: mostly associate with the junior ranks in Division Two.
1. Judge – partner not specified
2. Colonel – paired with Goliath Two (who can take Col.'s place if he is away)
3. General – paired with Goliath One the *man of lust*
4. Wireless Operator or Draad – paired with Silver One
5. Lieutenant/Germiston – paired with Silver Two

Senior Ranks in the Silver Line and their Sexual Partners
Division One in the Silver Line: has links to the probationers or has sexual contact with lower ranking members in the Silver Two Line.
1. The Governor General (Mtshali the Blacksmith) – has sex with Goliath One but can also have sex with any probationer.
2. The Doctor (Nyanga/Nyangi) – is paired with the Under Magistrate.
3. The Inspector (Glas/Mafotsha) – may only have sex with a non-28 because his work is mainly outside the camp.
4. The Clerk (Mabalang) – partner not recorded.
5. The Magistrate (Goba) – no designated partner, can use probationers.
6. The Under Magistrate (Landdros) – Schurink was told that this post is paired with the Doctor but then doubt was cast on the information; in October 2005 the identical information was provided *the under-magistrate's babba is the Nyangi*. This makes sense as the under-magistrate is described as having *a foot in both camps*. He has also moved up from the position of Goliath One who is 'euphemistically' known as *the whore of the 28 Camp*.

71

upgraded

Inter-gang myth states that to be promoted from a *wyfie* and achieve masculine status the gang member must prove himself and *take blood*, carry out a stabbing. It seems that this activity is more honoured in the omission than the observance. The *wyfies* are automatically upgraded to male status when they lose their looks. So all the talk of blood, violence and stabbing to become a man again — take it with a pinch of salt.

While stabbing of a warder will not be pre-arranged a *frans* who is stabbed is usually pre-warned and then bribed not to lay a charge after the event — bribed (or threatened) into saying he has no idea who stabbed him.

but is it rape?

When a man consents to being the subordinate partner, if he is not visibly forced and the sex is seemingly consensual, then the question of whether he was actually raped hangs in the air and remains unresolved. Coercion in a prison environment from powerful gang members is subtle and not that easy to define, but the consequences for a new inmate, who is unwilling to comply, will be sinister. If a man lacks the skills to qualify for membership of the 26s, if he is too fearful, or not given an opportunity to stab another and prove himself, if he has already been forced in the prison van to take a dagga poke in the anus (a parcel of dagga and drugs forcibly placed inside the body) or raped in the court cells and needs gang protection in prison, he is going to end up as a probationer and a *wyfie* even if he has heterosexual relationships outside of the prison.

His warders, to ease their conscience when they do nothing, will more than likely consider him a closet homosexual.

I enquired further about the dagga poke, although part of me did not really want to know: "Being forced to carry a dagga poke does not necessarily mean you cannot become one with the *Ouens van Sontop*, because it is not actually sodomy. The dagga poke is wrapped in plastic, it's about the size of a parcel of dagga. And, you know, dagga is like gold in prison, a small amount that fits onto the top of a twenty-cent coin, well that sells for ten rand. And most gangsters carry their own dagga (in the anus) or they can swallow it."

There was more: "If you can't get a *frans*, then you do it yourself. But if a *frans* refuses they make him. They take off his pants and then they use a bottle to kick the dagga up his arse. And then they watch him and if it does not come out then they put a plastic packet over the hand and they wrench it out and that guy, well there is lots of blood."

72

What other factors — apart from not being forced to carry a dagga poke and risk having his insides perforated — make a healthy, heterosexual male enter the Silver Line to become a designated female for the duration of his stay in prison?

Sometimes it is for camaraderie and support, to ban loneliness. Men comply out of hopelessness, knowing that the prison system cannot help them and the gang will get to them no matter where they are incarcerated. They will be protected against rape and violence from other inmates by their provider, their designated partner, whom they serve as a wife serves her husband. They are quartered with men in the same boat; their position is dignified with tasks and a uniform, even if their status is limited. There is always a chance that they will get promoted quickly and that the nightmare will end when they become recognised as men again.

Some insist: "You cannot survive in prison without the support of others."

Can a man be lured into the 28 Gang?

If a prisoner does not have the skills required by the 26 Gang he will be *spotted* by the Glas/Inspector who scouts for the 28 Gang and wooed with *benefits*.

Much of the success of the gangs is based on *mind power* — they are very persuasive speakers. They will make the new inmate an offer he may not be able to refuse. They will summon him into their presence and he is expected to be respectful. They will advertise the advantages of joining a gang. They will ask what he has heard about their particular branch of The Number and why he wants to join their *other* brothers and not them.

The 28 General laughed and gave me a sly look when he demonstrated how they went about it, how they enticed the new inmate with false promises and suggestions that, if he was sufficiently courageous, they would make him a member of the prestigious Gold Line.

They will try to convince him the 26s are just out to rob him: *"Djy sien, my bru, daai is 'n 26. As djy besoek kry dan vat hy al jou goed. Kom saam met ons en hou jou kroon. Is djy sterkbene, kan jy die bewaarders steek? Ons sal jou manskap maak van bloed."*

The 26s will tell him they are not interested in his cash or his visits, but they'd like to make his heart strong so that he can stand up for himself if he encounters problems. Sometimes the choice made will depend on whether the new inmate has friends in the gang, or if there are many from that gang in the area from which he comes.

Although warders hotly deny that men are lured by the 28s, possibly seeing it as a reflection of their own inadequacy, members of both the 26 Gang that I interviewed and members of the 28 Gang admitted that it did happen. Sasha Gear's research indicates that, yes, a man can be tricked without thinking, perhaps by accepting some luxury which he cannot afford, or allowing someone else to stand up for him. This will indicate a weakness and he will be allocated a subsidiary role, a role that declares he will perform favours for protection because he does not have the guts to fight.

It is easy to project criticism onto the warders for not preventing recruitment, but Correctional Services offers no information on the prison gangs when warders are trained, there is no overall policy that prison heads are encouraged to adopt towards the gangs, no protection for officers who prevent gang rituals and meagre alternatives for those prisoners who do not join gangs. Correctional Services operate as if the prison gangs do not exist.

The organised sexual arrangements made by the gang can possibly be viewed as one way of reducing aggression. However, it severely limits the options of any man who wishes to come to prison and serve his sentence without being made a victim of an iniquitous system.

In like manner the man who joins the Camp of 26 does not necessarily do it out of his own free will. Some were in-your-face honest, "I joined the 26s because I did not want to be fucked in the arse."

ranks, roles and glad rags

The gangs are outfitted in prison with clothing, weapons and accoutrements that exist only in their imagination. The invention of these invisible fantasy uniforms developed within the prison system when they were forbidden to alter their external appearance or carry weapons.

Members, in all three gangs, must recognise the uniform of their gang brothers and be able to describe their own uniform. This is particularly relevant when a gang member is transferred from another prison even though they do not take him at his word as to rank. Transferred members will be placed in quarantine for six, seven or eight *years* (days in actual time/depending on whether they are 26s, 27s or 28s) while information will be gathered regarding what uniform they really wear and whether they infringed gang law at the previous prison.

Today they use cell phones to find out what they want to know. The pieces are stored separately to prevent easy discovery and the phones are re-assembled after lock-up.

Gold Line/Division One

Division One wears gabardine with a gold book as a buckle and a gold book on their helmets and gold leg wrappings or puttees. The stars on the right shoulder are said to be *gold*, those on the left shoulder are *silver*.

1. **The Judge** displays seven gold and seven silver stars on his shoulders; when he hands down the death sentence or *the rope* he uses a black pen and has eight stars on each shoulder. He must oversee the sentence.

2. **The General** with six gold and six silver stars is able to issue weapons and declare war and he ensures that *a wrong is righted*. Before him is the *skoemba* (skin with the laws on it). His can be a straight promotion from the rank of soldier if he is particularly bloodthirsty. He is presented as a diabolical figure with a pitchfork and bloody face. At the ovens, in his role of blacksmith, he is dressed in a khaki overall with blood red shoes of iron and holds an assegai and pronged fork. He is wrapped in a blanket.

3. **The Colonel** with four gold and and four silver stars is in possession of the skin of the beast Rooiland on which the gang laws are written. He carries no weapons. He wears a bloodied gabardine uniform. He opens up the laws at the Twelve Points and is the lawgiver of the gang. He issues the ranks and uniforms and rations as well as punishments and must keep a tally of the number of men in the ranks on the blackboard. If The Number is slighted he is the one designated to stab a warder. He has a blood red car with grass green seats. He also holds the invisible post of Ntshotshisane, the spy, which indicates an awareness (in the subconscious of the gang) that their *piemp* was a high-ranking gang member. Nongoloza himself was the first member to disclose the gang's methods of operation and it's easy to speculate that this is his last post within the gang.

4. **The Wireless Operator** (Draad) has three gold and three silver stars, he is dressed in mustard coloured gabardine and wears a cap with a red band and red shoes. He carries a dagger at his right side. He is selected for his exceptional memory. When he speaks it is like switching on a tape-recorder. He is the *ears and eyes* of the gang and must be constantly aware of everything that is happening and informs of events in the Camp of 26 and 27, amongst warders and *franse* as well as amongst the latest intake. He has a bugle to call men to the Twelve Points when trouble brews. He is supposed to report on any problems with prison food. He carries red handcuffs and a 'skelm sleutel' or 'mischievous key'. (This humanising of the key blew me! I was told: "Every prisoner has the potential to own a *skelm sleutel* - a key that allows entry into an activity that is not legitimate.

He keeps it in his head, to work his way around the warders, so he can get to places he should not be. But the Draad's key, well that one is official. It's one of his attributes - excellent mind power - to get his post.") To keep him up to date with modern technology the Draad is issued with silver wires *to receive* and gold to *play back*.

5. **The Lieutenant** (Jim Crow the Germiston) – at Centre Post – has two gold and two silver stars. He wears gabardine, a cap with a red band and gold badge and red shoes. His shirt and jacket each have four gold buttons, fastened. He is armed with an assegai or bayonet. He controls the flow of information to the upper ranks and to those below him and so links Divison One, Soldiers and Privates. He is an expert on gang lore and tests the scholars. He stands watch at the Twelve Points. He escorts recruits in Section One to their initiation. He is also the pimp. He wears a white glove on one hand to deal with *wyfies* who cannot cope with blood and a red on the other for work in the Bloodline. He holds two silver keys for the women's camp and the *forties* (hospital and jail) and two gold keys for work in the Bloodline. He directs probationers (*wyfies*) for sexual purposes. He is also referred to as Amapint or the Pint Milk Bottle. The allusion being that the *wyfies* are empty regarding The Number until the Number Ones in the gang *make them full*.

Gold Line/Division Three

The Captains and Sergeants are taken from the ranks of the soldiers; they wear khaki uniforms stamped 28 with different insignia to indicate status.

1. **Captain One** displays 4 stripes on his uniform and his badge is a castle. He acts as general of the soldiers. His orders come from Division One through the Lieutenant. He disciplines for minor infringements.

2. **Captain Two** is indicated by his stripes and his rifle. He is in a complimentary position to the colonel in the upper ranks. He can throw open the *skoemba* (skin) and decides when they will *sit kring* (hold court) in Division Three at the Four Points.

3. **Sergeant One** displays 3 stripes and carries ammunition. He instructs new members in the laws and traditions of the camp. He is positioned at *the gate* to ensure soldiers do not abscond – go AWOL!

4. **Sergeant Two** displays 2 stripes, one pointing downwards. He carries a knapsack filled with tobacco for the wyfies. He is positioned at the *crossroads* and allocates tasks to those who wish to join. He is the jailer when offences are committed and he escorts men to the Four Points. As drill sergeant he also inspects the troops and issues orders.

Soldiers in the Camp of Twenty-Eight

The soldiers (masjallou) are dressed completely in khaki with three gold buttons on their jackets – the top button left undone to indicate a constant readiness for work – they are issued with red boots and golden gaiters, khaki helmets (bearing a badge representing a lion's head), and are armed with an assegai and .303. They are issued with eight golden bullets – seven in the magazine and one in the firing-chamber and a bag with an additional 20 gold bullets. They are expressly forbidden any contact with the probationers or *wyfies*. Their role is to protect the wyfies' camp –The House of Moliva – for twenty-four hours a day. They do sentry duty at night to be on the alert for the arrival of a warder.

the shadow cabinet

The Silver Line

The colour green is worn by officers in the private line, unless they are called to fight — then they wear gabardine. The exception is the public prosecutor who is dressed as a probationer but with a green stripe on his clothing. (This clothing more than corroborates his role as *wyfie* to the Nyangi.) The magistrate, doctor and clerk from this division serve at the Twelve Points. A change in circumstances requires a change in clothing. A man cannot go *agter die berge* to the isolation cells (punishment by prison authorities) wearing green, he must change into his khaki uniform.

Silver Line/Division One

1. **The Governor General** with seven gold and seven silver stars, sometimes referred to as The Government, keeps *the skin*, the Book of Laws, and hands down the law. He is responsible for issuing provisions such as tobacco. As *the stairs* he can be called to the Twelve Points if there are problems with *Government Issue*, including the issuing of imaginary clothing.

2. **The Doctor** with six gold and six silver stars and a white jacket over his clothing, ensures there are no suspicious marks on the knives at general meetings – *wat op 'n lokval (trap) kan dui*. He issues the knife (real this time!) – depending on the type of wound to be inflicted. He examines newcomers to the gang for *dirty marks* (tattoos) that indicate they already have a gang allegiance and could have been sent as spies. He works with the sick and injured in *the forties*. He is responsible for all medical matters. He tastes the food to see if it has been poisoned or served *met poison of salute*. Most important: he examines new recruits to decide whether their hearts beat *twice, thrice, once* a year, thus determining their prison careers

— *two* beats indicates a *wyfie*, *three/one* Gold Line. In keeping with modern medicine he has a choice of practising either with a stethoscope or the entrails of an animal (as would the sangoma in African tradition) and has a red cross displayed on each shoulder and on his briefcase — which is green outside and pure white within and contains twelve *mabopas* or pipes (presumably stethoscopes). He drives a grass green wagon with three gold wheels, but the fourth is up in the air. (I never found out why!) He works himself out of the *wyfies* by stabbing an unfortunate warder to take blood.

3. **The Inspector** (Glas), with his binoculars, sees far and wide and has six gold and six silver stars, a uniform stamped inside and out with the number 28 and an axe to clear the bush to reach the new inmates. He makes sure the men are well schooled in gang mythology and plays a role when promotion occurs. He spies out the land to recruit new members and escorts the *franse* from the bush to the camp of 28. He carries a bunch of keys (15) and with his *skelm key* he can open any place in the Camp of 28. He walks with the Wireless Operator (Draad) and they give witness for each other. They will, for example, escort a man who has been ordered to perform a *duty*, which could include the stabbing of a warder and they ensure the duty is carried out to the letter. Die Glas communicates with the other gangs and the warders and must be informed if a gang member has to speak to a warder. He reports to the Twelve Points and makes sure that anyone who sits at the Twelve Points is a genuine 28, but the Glas is not himself a member of the Twelve Points. He inspects the private line. He stabs to get rank – *het sy rang afgeskiet*.

4. **The Clerk** (Rwenza is another word used for this post in the Western Cape) with four gold and four silver stars is both secretary and accountant. He carries a set of pens used in the same manner as the magistrate's stamps. He also schools privates.

5. **The Magistrate** with three gold and three silver stars, clothing stamped with 28 and four silver buttons tightly done up, hands down punishments for minor infringements and he also sits at the Twelve Points. The stamps: *red* for blood, if an offence is proved; *green* if the case is thrown out of court or if a privilege is awarded; *white* if it is a probationer's case discussed in Division One; *black* indicates a death sentence.

6. **The Public Prosecutor**, similar to the Lieutenant, is also described as having *a foot in two camps* as he plays a mediator's role in relation to the Number Ones above him and in relation to those in the camp below. He displays two stars on each shoulder. His four silver buttons are always fastened. He carries a white satchel with a green lining. He wears gabardine

if required to fight, but otherwise dresses as a private, in white shorts with a green stripe and a head scarf (sometimes called a bonnet) with a green stripe. He carries a cane and, apart from the stars on his shoulders, he will have a cross tattooed on his body. He is promoted from the privates, the *wyfies*, and was Goliath One (the camp whore) before he attained this position. He docks the tails (*hy kap hulle sterte*) of the *wyfies* (takes privileges away) – makes sure they do not initiate male sexual acts as they have been selected for light work. He is expected to tick off the privates at the Four Points and divert serious cases to the Lieutenant. He protects the *wyfies* (in theory) from being sodomised by non-28 gang members.

the proletariat
Silver Line/Division Two
All ranks in this line wear the same white uniform as the probationers but embellished with a green stripe. It is their role to look after the kraal.
1. **Goliath One is Magubaan**, the female head of the privates, who appears at the Twelve Points when a private commits a serious offence; he can go wherever he will in the camp and have sex with anyone he pleases, he is not reliant on the Lieutenant to direct him. His white clothing is decorated with green stripes and his white handkerchief is tied to his left pulse. He carries the imprint of a red star on his forehead to indicate that he was injured in the battle between Nongoloza and Ngilikityane and possibly to verify that he was originally one of Ngilikityane's men. In African tradition he waves a beast's tail in his right hand to cool down the blood-mad general at the Twelve Points. When the death sentence is handed down it is Goliath One who strips and dances naked to fill the heads of those at the Twelve Points with lustful thoughts. The victim's sentence is then commuted to gang rape. Goliath One is usually chosen for his youth and good looks and is described as the whore of the 28s who can work the men up into a sexual frenzy. He must be *believable as a woman*. If there is no General to discipline a culprit then Magubaan (the General's child) is General at The Points. If he removes his clothes then koppe sak (heads are bowed); if the culprit is given a duty that lands him in solitary confinement then, on release, he must have sex with Magubaan and this means he rises in rank. Sexual rituals take place in the Queens Bed (this is a Silver Line term only) when the sheets are hung up to exclude prying eyes.
2. **Goliath Two** carries *two* keys and gives the laws to the privates. The Colonel is responsible for seeing that he *works himself up* into a superior position.

3. **Silver One** (Masilva) with *one* key chides the underachievers. His personal *babba* (The Wireless Operator) is responsible for him.

4. **Silver Two** (Masilva) is given *two* keys and a piece of chalk to count and record the number of probationers. His keys open the gates. During his period of training he is *tolomhlophe* (he cannot have sex in camp as he has no ngunyas, but he has the authority to rape a *frans*) and the Landdros takes him and they build him under The Ones and he *downs* at The Ones. (He is a reserve in terms of sexual activity.) He cannot be ordered to commit a bloody deed or be expected to fight. He is found in the deep level of The Twos with the probationers. He schools the probationers in a group (opens the book for them and protects them) as well as those up to Goliath One. Anyone identified by the Silver Two as possessing potential is elevated and given a *post-matric* so to speak. Silver Two will take the selected one to the Four Points where he will be scrutinised and tested for his insight; to build for the future and to make sure that those with brains do not get bored. This is an important task and is probably why the 28s will say you *get your true identity from the Silver Two*. He ensures the probationers observe the rules: *I will respect my brother, I must not swear at my brother, I must not lie to my brother, any information outside the camp that concerns the camp I must notify my Silver Two.*

Probationers/Division Two
This is the lowest rank in the private line. They are issued with white takkies (sandshoes) stamped in and out with the number 28, white socks and white shorts, a white belt with a silver buckle stamped 28 inside and out, a white shirt stamped 28 inside and out, a white jacket with two silver buttons (the top button left undone to show they are always available for work/sex), and a white headscarf (*doek*), with a silver badge stamped 28 inside and out and a white handkerchief to carry in the right-hand stamped 28 inside and out. The handkerchief is symbolic: to wipe themselves dry after they have been used as women. They wear the Moliva Boy tattoo on the left shoulder. They are directed in their activities by the Lieutenant. As *wyfies* they are never expected to fight and remain pampered and protected. They are kept cloistered in the Deep Level, sometimes referred to as *die stalle*.

📖

When any member of The Number leaves prison he hands in his uniform and rank. It is replaced with a *piece of the Number*, something to help the parolee survive outside. Maybe money, possibly an address of someone he can contact, maybe a tip-off as to where he can commit an easy crime!

Chapter Ten

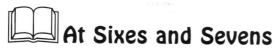 At Sixes and Sevens

the structure, roles, relationships and uniforms in the judicial, civil and military hierarchy of the 26 Gang

introduction

I was informed: "It isn't necessary to get a visit to be a benefit. The 26 Gang is looking for someone who can *skarra* (from Afrikaans for scavenge) and *jikijela* (eyes are everywhere), who has his wits about him wherever he is. Not a prisoner who just wants to get on with his own business and lie on his bunk and sleep all day (light work). It is someone who can look out for the gang, pick up any bits and pieces along the way, who can strengthen us here in the prison."

The Camp of 26 describe their role as *keeping the jail alive* — they are responsible for acquiring supplies of money, drugs, cigarettes and luxuries and for beating the system. They bring wealth to the prison and this must be shared with the Camp of 28 if they are low on resources.

"You know, the 28 and 27 are very similar, because at the beginning they got the same schooling. Remember the 27s also have a pot of blood and the head of their camp is also called The Lord. If you are a 28 and not a *wyfie* you can become a 27 by taking blood. Lots of blood."

The organisational structure of the Camp of 26 seems, at first glance, far simpler to analyse than that of the Camp of 28. When an attempt is made to unravel the symbiotic relationship with the Camp of 27 then it's gridlock! There are those in the ranks of 26 (General One, Madakeni, Captain One, Sgt. Major, Sgt. One, Sgt. Two, Nogidela) who also have the status of a 27 and *sit at The Points* of the Camp of Twenty-Seven when a quorum cannot be reached.

The Camp of 26 is considered by many to be a soft option when it comes to violence. However, there is evidence of their aggression in the mythical stories they tell each other.

"We killed to get the ranks. We murdered. We killed a judge who visited the prison to merit the rank. Likewise a general, captain etc. We had to kill the original office bearers to deserve the uniforms of judge, general, clerk in the Camp of 26."

Up until about 1998 it was still mandatory for a 26 to stab or slice a *vuil frans* (one who had reported on the gang to the warders) to obtain a rank.

It was the 26 Gang who were the victors of the bloody wars at Bellville Prison in 1967 and likewise at Brandvlei in 1974-6; wars sparked by a general election of senior gang members. As the 27s dwindle in numbers it is up to the soldiers of the Camp of Twenty-Six to do the fighting when the gangs declare war.

There is no ritual sex in the Camp of 26 or 27. Traditionally, as the *Ouens van Sontop*, they carry out their work between sunrise and sunset, while the Camp of 28 operates after sunset.

The Camp of Twenty-Six is divided into two sections. The unarmed privates sitting at the Twelve Points are referred to as Number Ones. Their position is mirrored by the officers known as Number Twos. The Camp is further described as sectioned off with privates in both the 26 and 27 Camp but with certain officers from the Camp of 26 also serving in the Camp of 27. At any stage a Twenty-Six may convert to the status of a Twenty-Seven for the purpose of communicating with the Camp of Twenty-Eight *vir die minute* or for the moment. If the 26 wants to retain his 27 status he must take blood. All ritual stabbings are observed by the Glas (Inspector) and the Draad or Wireless Operator (alternatively the Transistor Radio – for those identifying with the Twentieth Century) who will accompany the member who is designated to stab. This mirrors the procedure in the Camp of Twenty-Eight.

When a member of the Twenty-Six Camp becomes too aggressive he must take the status of a Twenty-Seven because *there is nowhere else for him to go* and he cannot co-exist within the Camp of Twenty-Six. Twenty-Six members should not look for blood and neither should they seek same-sex relationships.

Anyone who has been raped may not be a Twenty-Six. They use rape as a means of excluding members who have seriously offended the code of the 26 Gang. Same-sex activity in the Camp of Twenty-Six is, if it occurs, always concealed and never overt. Nor can anyone who has sustained a head injury while in prison remain a Twenty-Six unless he takes back his blood by stabbing a warder. During punishment rituals in the Camp of Twenty-Six there is a specific injunction against hitting the victim on the head. The ghost of Magubaan, the whore with the head wound whom Ngilikityane banished from his sight, hangs over the 26s.

If a man is raped as a Twenty-Six *duty* he then lives in fear of being stabbed in the head. This would mean his total exclusion from The Camp (the following up of the rape with a stab wound indicates that the rape did happen) or he could, if exposed by two of his brothers, be required to stab a warder — thereby getting an additional sentence on top of the one he is serving. (Of course, if he does prove himself by stabbing a warder, he acquires status and power: "If you stab a warder then you rule!")

These days most raped men avoid having to stab to cleanse themselves and as a result they almost cease to exist, they are left in limbo until some other Twenty-Six has to prove himself by challenging them. While in limbo they may still belong to The Camp but are humiliated by being banned from sitting in the circle, they may not *down in die kring* (sit on their haunches in the traditional manner while issues of importance to The Number are discussed and debated) but must sit apart as suspect and *down* on their own. Other members will be warned to avoid them and they will not be kept informed of the gang's activities. The latter is considered a great hardship. It is a form of living death. These men are ostracised (much as a cult punishes members who break the rules) by those from whom they previously received all their affirmation and this continues until they are prepared to defend their position and *take blood* with violence. It is an unenviable position. The victims are reduced to the status of *franse* or even worse, they no longer have any viable options. They never know when they will be stabbed, possibly fatally, by a brother performing *his duty*. Their nightmare is being absorbed into the *wyfies* of the Twenty-Eight Gang. They lose all privileges and are taunted with comments such as: "Give us a piece of your backside!"

The lesson is obvious: The Number can raise you up, but also bring you down with the removal of your rank and power.

When examining the detail of the Camp of Twenty-Six one notes that there is nothing grotesque about the costumes worn by the senior members – no blood-speckled faces, no old dry bloodstains on their uniforms – it's far more reality based. On the surface it appears more moderate, more civilised, almost clinical in comparison with the 28s.

The 26 dress code mirrors the uniform of the British soldiers during the Boer War. When a man is armed in the Camp of Twenty-Six it is said he is *geBritish*. When the gangs go to war then the soldiers are called. They are fully armed by Madakeni and stand in a circle to guard the Twelve Points. That is when the thin red line appears on the pure white flag of 26 alongside the dollar sign.

One should never lose sight of the thin red line on the pure white flag of the Camp of Twenty-Six which, by its magical appearance, gives permission for the 27s to come to the 26s and for the 26s to be armed for the purpose of shedding blood.

Rank and Rigmarole

Within the Camp of 26 the clothing is similar across the board with different insignia to indicate rank. The soldiers on the ground wear khaki, the non-combatants wear private clothing and the three senior ranks in The Twos (Madakeni/Sergeant Major/Die Draad) wear gabardine (twill-cloth). The 27 wears gabardine, his legs red with blood.

Ishumielnambini of the Ones

The Twelve Points deal with major issues. They sit judgement on cases where a stabbing has taken place between gang members (if his *gedagte is rooi*) and they pronounce on disputes in the gang. They act in an advisory and monitoring capacity, much like chief executive officers or directors of companies. The Twos must inform them of decisions made at the Twelve Points of The Twos.

1. **General** (Blackboard of the Ones) with 12 stars who is knowledgeable about the law.
2. **Inspector One** issues uniforms to new recruits alongside Captain One who escorts the novice to Nogidela at the Gates of Sunrise of the Camp 26; he ensures that punishments are carried out and is a dangerous man to cross.
3. **Doctor One**
4. **Clerk** (Mabalaan/Mcobozi)
5. **Advocate** (Mehli)
6. **Judge**

Captain One is **Captain of the Blood** with six stars. He comes from *skombizo* (The Sevens) with permission to steek or stab. He sits outside The Points.

The privates in the first line are only armed with the permission of Madakeni (The Fighting General) otherwise they carry sticks and briefcases and not weapons of war.

Ishumielnambini of the Twos

The Twelve Points of The Twos deal with the initiation of new recruits.

1. **The Fighting General** (Madakeni)
2. **The Inspector** (Mafotcha/Die Glas or Binoculars)
3. **The Doctor Two** (Nyanga/Nyangi)
4. **The Judge Number Two**
5. **The Lawyer** (Mehli)
6. **The Scribe** (Mcobozi)

Captain Two (The Draad/Wireless Operator) sits outside The Points. He merits four stars. He is worked up quickly from the soldiers and *hy's geBritish* (armed). He is there to help Madakeni search at The Points and searches new recruits at initiation. He is dressed in gabardine including a gabardine hat with a pure white band and the insignia of the red line, 26 and a coin; he wears brown boots with pure white puttees with insignia and six buckles, and is armed with a *bayonet* (sword) and revolver. He carries a pure white radio transmitter in his right hand stamped with his rank as well as a pure white swagger stick, which is also stamped. He has four stars, two on each shoulder. He is selected for his phenomenal memory. He memorises decisions taken at inter-gang meetings as well as being an observer and recorder at the Twelve Points. He carries a *special* book and pens.

Delineation of Roles, Status, Clothing and Gear

General Number Two (The Fighting General) is also known as Die Band and as Madakeni (sometime mispronounced by Afrikaans speaking inmates as *Madagunee*) and he comes from The Sevens. He ratifies the insignias of each particular office. He is recognised by his eight stars, four on each shoulder and a red band on his arm inscribed with *Fighting in the Camp of Twenty-Six*. He confers promotion with the agreement of his executive officers and ratifies the insignia on the uniform of the new recruits. He wears brown boots stamped inside and out with the number 26, pure white puttees with a thin red line and stamped 26 and six buckles - three on each side. He wears gabardine pants and jacket with six pure white buttons stamped 26 and a red line, he has a bayonet on the left side (with the pure white *handvastel* stamped 26 and a thin red line); on his right side he carries a loaded revolver in a brown holster – six bullets, one in the firing chamber. He wears a gabardine cap with a pure white band also stamped 26 and with a thin red line. He has a pure white *special* book with a thin red line and stamped 26; a black pen to record wrongs and a white pen to record right. His role is similar to that of the Blacksmith in the 28 Camp, he has a knife at the Twelve Points and he hands out the weapons of war when the privates must be armed. He also has the role of The Blackboard and schools those above (Number Ones) and those below. He wields much power and gives instructions to Inspector Two, Nyangi Two, Mehli, Judge and Mcobozi. At the Twelve Points everyone *downs* — Madakeni with a knife and everyone else with thumbs-up in the salute of 26. It is The Fighting General Madakeni who gives the order for the One-Time Shot Gun which opens proceedings at the Twelve Points and for the Two-Time Shot Gun which give the Nyangi permission to swear in the new recruit.

Inspector Two (Mafotcha or Die Glas) is responsible for seeing duties are performed and lessons learned and so plays a significant role in the promotion of members. He goes unarmed and wears private shoes stamped inside and out with 26 and private pants and jacket with six pure white buttons; he carries a pure white set of books (he sees inside everybody's head) with a thin red line and stamped Mafotcha 2; a pure white badge with a thin red line is displayed on his right upper-lapel and is also stamped Mafotcha 2; he wears a private cap with a pure white band and a red line and stamped with a coin and 26. He also carries a *special* book.

The Nyangi/Doctor examines the new recruit, looking at his eyes and ears and testing his strength as he parodies a military medical examination. He then instructs the recruit to hold out his arm which he bends back until hand touches shoulder, the solemn oath is then administered and the new recruit sworn in while everyone else *downs* at The Points. The Nyangi is unarmed and similarly attired to the Mafotcha and also carries a *boek stelsel* but his stamp states Nyangi. The Doctor also declares men fit to drill.

Judge Number Two sits for minor cases and is dressed like the Mafotcha and not armed. He has a pure white set of books in his right hand, with a thin red line and stamped (*stalala coboza*) Judge Two; likewise his badge, worn on the right lapel. He oversees the sentence passed.

Mehli the Lawyer pleads on behalf of the offender. He is dressed like Mafotcha and not armed and carries a set of books and a badge, both stamped with his rank.

Mcobozi the Scribe is both a secretary and an accountant. He is dressed in similar garb to the Mafotcha, goes unarmed and carries a set of books and badge.

Rock and Role

1. **Sergeant Major:** his role is to ensure discipline is maintained amongst the troops and he can imprison inmates in his own jail prior to sentencing. He wears three stripes and one star and is similarly attired to the Draad, wearing gabardine. He is armed with bayonet and revolver. He has a *special* book and pens.

2. **Sergeant One:** he manages the store including munitions and (invisible) uniforms. He wears khaki, has three stripes that point upwards and is armed with bayonet (sword) and revolver and a *special* book with the usual insignia. He escorts the new recruit to the Number Ones where, in the presence of Inspector One, he will be issued with his uniform.

3. **Sergeant Two:** he is the drill sergeant who tells the new recruits *you will drill every six years* (this usually happens in the bathroom area); he demonstrates the correct manoeuvres *to down* at The Points; he escorts the new recruit from Nogidela to Sergeant One. He wears khaki with the usual stamps and has two stripes that face upwards indicating where his orders emanate from. He is armed with bayonet and a revolver and carries a *special* book.

4. **Nogidela:** he takes the recruit at the gate from Glas and Cpt.One and hands him into the care of Sgt. Two. He is the soldiers' teacher of the law/history of the 26s. He gives permission for special leave, or tattoos etc. In prison he schools the soldiers with six works *of which he will speak only of four, the other two honour The Number.* (Those with rank go to The Number Ones and Twos to be schooled.) On the 6th day (Saturday) the soldiers and their Nogidela get a visit from Glas and Draad who test them. Nogidela is also the Gatesman (keeping tally of the troops); he guards the port of entry and exit. He records the money available to them and the *gebruike* — the luxuries and drugs and cigarettes. He is dressed in khaki with similar insignia to the soldiers below him but is armed with bayonet and revolver. He wears one stripe on the upper arm of his jacket which points downwards to indicate that he schools those below him. He carries, as the Gatesman, 25 keys at his right side and the 26th key is the master key in his right-hand; 6 keys are for the soldiers and 19 for the ranks. He informs the recruit of his duty to guard the camp and to look for a *kroon* or anything that will be of benefit to the camp.

87

Soldiers in the Camp of Twenty-Six are armed and ready 24/7

Prior to initiation the novice is met outside the Camp and is escorted to Nogidela by Captain One and Inspector One and left at the Gates of Sunrise; while being observed in the bush (in prison) for suitability he is issued with khaki overalls and boots without laces and a pick and a spade (minus insignia) — his trench tools. During this period he is taught the first pages of the oral code from the Book of 26 so that he is protected from being sodomised by the 28s. Once initiated at the Twelve Points the soldier wears brown boots stamped inside and out with the number 26, pure white puttees (strip of cloth wound around the leg for support) with a thin red line and stamped 26, six buckles (three on each side), khaki pants and khaki jacket with six pure white buttons with a thin red line and stamped 26; he carries a bayonet with a pure white handle – with a thin red line and stamped 26 – at his left side; he is armed with a .303 (gun of the British army) held against the right shoulder and provided with 26 bullets (twenty-five in the magazine and one in the firing-chamber); he is issued with a khaki helmet with a pure white band with a thin red line stamped with a coin and the number 26. He too must carry a pure white *special* book with 26 pure white pages each with a thin red line *kroon en nommer gestam 26.* He is given a black pen for wrongs and a white pen to record *the rights.*

Once again I wanted to know what was so special about the 'special book' and the pens that all the 26s carry.

"It's in your head, the *special book* is your brain, your memory and how you use it!"

"Oh!" there was not much more I could say.

They are encouraged to spy on their brothers and to report misdeeds and this is what the black pen is used for.

"If there is a problem then we *down with a black pen* and, when a solution has been arrived at, we *rise with a white pen.* If you must stab then the *black pen is used to write into the thin red line* on the flag of 26."

Saturday, *die Sesde Jaar* is a big day! It's duty day and parliament meets and Glas and Draad go to the deep level (to the soldiers) to *jikijela* (search their heads for knowledge).

This happens at every prison in the country on every Saturday of the month.

initiation rites and rituals

The initiation rituals of all three camps are similar in nature; except there is no sexual initiation in the Camp of 26 and 27.

Both Nogidela and Madakeni play important roles during initiation in the Camp of 26. The names Nogidela and Madakeni are throwbacks to the African origins of The Number. Nogidela is the Captain of the Dance in African culture. He stands in front of the *impi* (the regiment of soldiers) and demonstrates the moves. He would *rev* the warriors up before battle with his frenzied dancing and singing; an important psychological tactic.

The title of Madakeni for the Fighting General initially puzzled me. Madakeni, coming from the Zulu word *mdaka*, indicates mud or dirt; *umadakeni* means black. By inference it seemed *madakeni* meant a muddy place. Exploring further I discovered that those of high rank in Zulu society wear *a brass armband* on the upper arm called a *mdaka*. Hence *Madakeni* or *Die Band* (a nickname) is a title assumed by the Fighting General to indicate his position of honour. His blood-red band worn on the upper arm is inscribed with: *Fighting in the Camp of 26.*

📖

What follows is an abridged (in that the repetition is left out) translation (from Afrikaans/Zulu/Xhosa) of the initiation of a 26 at *Ishumielnambini* (Twelve Points). The procedure is recorded in full and in the vernacular in the addendum to *God's Gangsters?* The recruits learn to recite this procedure orally after their initiation so that, when elevated to a higher rank, they will ensure that tradition is strictly adhered to. Prior to learning the initiation procedures members of all three Camps must be able to recite The Homecoming (see page 132).

initiation in the Camp of 26

The recruits *wait in the bush* while the Twelve Points of the Twos are constituted. The members of the Twelve Points sit in a circle around the white flag with some coins scattered upon it to commemorate the original six. This is a most solemn ceremony. All the 26 members must bear witness and the cell bunks are reorganised to give the gang as much space as possible. Non-members must sit in silence with their faces to the wall. The other Number Gangs will have already received formal notification that an initiation is going to take place.

When the Twelve Points are ready the new recruit is led to the Gates of Sunrise where Nogidela guards the soldiers who sit between him and Sgt. Two. The new recruit is marched in military fashion (everyone else standing at attention) past Sgt. Two (who demonstrates how the recruit should *down* at The Points) and Sgt. One (to be issued with his uniform by Inspector One) before being paraded in front of the Sgt. Major who arrests him for six minutes until Captain Two (The Draad) arrives to release him and escort him to The Twelve Points and into the presence of Madakeni, Inspector Two, the Doctor, the Lawyer, the Judge and the Scribe.

The new recruit must be acknowledged by all present and he himself must remain totally humble and claim ignorance of all that he is shown until he is enlightened. Any cockiness and he is out on his ear!

'At the sixth moment a man (Die Draad/Wireless Operator) appeared with four stars, two on each shoulder: He lifted his right thumb in salute and said: *"Salute, Sgt Major! Soos my drade gegrens word* (as I protect/monitor the boundaries), *I have come to release this malighta* (one of the alternative names given to the Ninevites prior to 1910) *who is called to The Points, hy is baitela voor jou stokkies* (temporarily locked up/waiting in your lock-up), *ek phakamisa hom chaisana."* (*chaisana* is talk and *phakamisa* is used frequently to indicate that The Number is being strengthened or raised up/the sense here being: 'I propose him as okay!')

Sgt. Major returned the salute and then Captain Two with the Four Stars, well he took me into the presence of the pure-white flag where I saw six men sitting with their heads close together. It was then that Captain Two searched me for any weapons with which I could injure the company before me. Captain Two lifted his right thumb and said: *"Salute, Madakeni!"*

I saw a man stand up with Eight Stars, four on each shoulder and Captain Two again addressed this man, saying: *"Salute! Here is the youngster the Twelve Points have summoned into their presence."* Madakeni, the Fighting General of the 26s (for indeed it was he) stood up and announced: *"Salute, Captain Two! You have accomplished your task well, now stand back and take up your position at your pure-white post."*

"Salute!" responded Captain Two.

Madakeni, the Fighting General of the Twos, then confronted me and asked: *"Do you know whose ground you stand upon?"*

"Nakanye!" I answered.

"You stand on the full-ground of Twenty-Six."

Madakeni then showed me I must salute and *down*: *"Do you know where you down?"* (The humbling of a person, avoiding eye-contact and kneeling before a superior is very much part of African culture.)

"Nakanye!" I answered. (The new recruit crouches down and follows instructions and continues to plead ignorance of where he is.)

And Madakeni (Die Band) cautioned me and again addressed me: *"You down on the full-ground of the Twelve Points in the Camp of Twenty-Six. Here there is a gate to enter by, but none by which you may leave. And to this place we invite no person, nor do we chase anyone away. Did you arrive here on your own two legs, with a true heart and complete understanding?"*

"Salute! Ja."

"Will your legs always be strong to carry out the tasks of the People of the Sun Rise." (Ouens van Sonop)

"Salute! Yes."

"Then, good, we will now gcwalisela en gcina (gwalisela means make complete/fill up and *gcina* is do/perform/keep The Number) *with a One-Time Shotgun to allow the first man at my right-hand, the Inspector, to give him the full power to complete his tasks."*

"Salute!"

"Stand up! One-Time Shotgun! Salute Inspector!"

(They perform the One-Time Shotgun to begin the ceremony - p.64)

The man at Madakeni's right-side, Inspector Number Two (Die Glas), the first man, inspected my body closely for *vuil brandmerke van ander nasies, van verre lande* (filthy marks belonging to other nations/tattoos representing other gangs in countries far away). When finished Inspector Two raised his right thumb in a salute: *"Salute, Madakeni!"*

Madakeni placed me at his right-hand side and ordered me: *"Salute, down!"*

He questioned Die Glas: *"Hosh, Mafotcha, what can you now inform us in accordance with the glass with which you searched this man?"*

"My glass changed to pure white and I phakamisa Twenty-Six."

After Die Glas had acknowledged me as a suitable Twenty-Six soldier each member of the Twelve Points of The Twos was called upon to verify what Mafotcha (Die Glas/ the Inspector Two) had ascertained, so that I was acknowledged suitable by *all* present. (This safeguards any arguments later on — that someone was recruited without full agreement.)

When this was over Madakeni spoke again: *"Fondela* (know) *soos Die Nommer phakamisa* (also translates as proposes/proclaims) *ek ook phakamisa Twenty-Six. I propose this man as a Twenty-Six. Now we will stand and gcina with a Two-Time Shotgun to give my second right-hand man the full power to complete his tasks. Salute up! Two-Time Shotgun!"*

91

When the formalities of the Two-Time Shotgun had been completed then the Nyanga took out his pipes (mabobas/stethoscope) to examine me (including my eyes and ears) and to see if I was fit. He asked me if I suffered from any illness, sickness or disability.

"*Nakanye!*"

Nyanga enquired: "*Can you hear (tola) and see (fotcha) and salute?*"

And I showed him: "*Salute!*"

(The Nyanga, similar to a sangoma – traditional doctor/healer is the person who administers, in the presence of the full camp and Twelve Points of the Twos, the solemn oath that binds the recruit to The Number for the rest of his life.)

the oath of 26 is administered

Nyanga spoke: "*Now I take the lewende stam* (living stem or stamp) *of Twenty-Six and I burn it into your bomvana* (veins). *I take your strength and I break it and I divide it up in the Camp of Twenty-Six. Remember, you are not stronger than your brother* (the next man) *nor is he stronger than you. You are shown and given a fourth eye to gcina* (to do/carry out/to keep watch). *There where your brother cannot see or hear you will see and hear and where you cannot see and hear he will keep a look out. If you ever get tired of doing the work of this house I will come to fetch the stamp (26) and take your blood as forfeit.*"

As he spoke I extended both my arms and the Nyanga examined my palms and then he took my right hand and he bent my arm (so breaking my power) until my hand touched my shoulder. Then, his task completed, Nyanga turned to Madakeni and said: "*Salute, Madakeni!*"

Then Madakeni motioned me to salute and *down*.

Madakeni then asked the doctor (Nyanga) to state what he had found and Nyanga replied: "*Ek, Nyanga, soos ek my mabobas gestel het, het dit fit gechange daai nobangela ek phakamisa Stupa.*"(I, Nyanga, consulted my pipes and find this man fit to be a 26.)

Then the Number Twos at the Twelve Points were asked each in their turn to verify what the Nyanga had found — that I was a suitable newcomer to the Camp of Twenty-Six.

After the oath was administered Madakeni made his speech and gave me my rank, insignia and weapons. Madakeni introduced me, his new soldier, to all the ranks at the Twelve Points and the uniform of each rank was described. I was told that, from this moment onwards, I was to recognise Madakeni himself by the blood-red band he wore on his upper right-arm inscribed with the motto Fighting in the Camp of Twenty-Six.'

the initiation speech of Madakeni

"Listen well, now you are a madoda (man) and the things of a frans (innocent prisoner) *you have left in the bush.* (This mirrors, to a certain extent, the initiation rites of the Xhosa male.) *I give you the right to salute with your right thumb, to look for a kroon (money) and to speak the madoda's language, the sabela. You are given twenty-six laws, but you only sabela six.* (The reference to twenty-six laws is a convention that Completes the Number, there are, in fact, only six laws to be obeyed.) *(1)You will not do as you please; (2)you will not talk behind your brother's back; (3)you will not lie to your brother; (4)a new prisoner you will warn twice and the third time The Number will show you how to deal with him; (5)the cops clean work* (the legitimate work of the warders in handing out food/seeing to lock up procedures etc) *you will respect but not his dirty work* (if the warders interfere in the work of The Number then you do not co-operate with the warders); *(6)you stand with your brother nomakanjani die nobangela* (no matter what the reason/result). *En jy sal met you broer vedala onder daai spierwit vlag nomakanjani hoe die nobangela lyk.* (You will stand alongside your brother under the pure white flag and complete what must be done no matter what the reason/even if it looks wrong/dangerous to you/ even if you die.) *You will be given six tasks of which you will sabela four and two is op slasluka. You will be given tasks, but I am not the person who will school you in those tasks. There is a man in die lyn van Die Nommer* (ranks of The Number) *who will school you. From now on I will fondela* (know) *you as a full-force soldier in The Camp of Stupa* (six in Zulu is isithupa). *I will know you by your pair of brown boots, stamped inside and out with the number 26; a pair of pure-white puttees inscribed with a thin red line and the stamp of Stupa and six buckles three on each side; your khaki pants and khaki jacket with six pure-white buttons each button bearing a thin red line and embossed with the stamp Stupa; bayonet at your left side with a pure-white handle, decorated with a thin red line and the stamp Stupa; a .303 over your right shoulder with 26 bullets, 25 in the magazine and one in the barrel. Twenty-six volgens Nommer! I will recognise you by your khaki helmet, pure-white band with a thin red line stamped with the mark of a coin and 26; by your pure-white special book with 26 pure-white pages each page with a thin red line and stamped 26; by your black pen and white pen, black for wrong and white for right. And that is how, from this moment onwards, I will acknowledge you in the Camp of Twenty-Six as a full-force soldier!"*

When he had finished his speech Madakeni asked each member of The Points to testify as to what he had witnessed. Mcobozi stated that he had written me into his book as a *full-force soldier* and offered a general salute. Madakeni then ordered me to take up my post. He called for Captain Two: *"I, Madakeni, phakamisa ook met die werk van die Twaalf Punte. Wat die werke met salute gepikelela* (goes) *het dan sal ek die manskap opspeel met lyn van nommer tot op sy spierwit pos.* (I will recognise him in his assigned/lawful rank exactly as The Number prescribes.) *Hosh, Kaptein, gcwala die Twaalf Punte het met salute sy werk gedala* (The Points have concluded their work in accordance with the rules of 26) *en die manskap sal jy fondela as a full-force soldier in the Camp of 26* (you will recognise this man as a full 26) *en ek phakamisa jy moet hom opspeel met lyn van nommer* (reel him in, take him in charge and teach him his duties in the pure tradition of the Number) *tot op sy spierwit pos."*

The Captain then identified himself to me as Die Draad and handed me over to the Sgt. Major who acknowledged me and handed me in turn to Sgt. One who, in his turn, handed me over to Sgt. Two whose role it was to take me to Nogidela, the teacher and supervisor of all the soldiers in the Camp of Twenty-Six. Nogidela accepted me and I *downed* (in respect) before my teacher and before the full school of Nogidela. I was reminded of the rules laid down by Madakeni and Nogidela showed me his 19 keys and his master-key and repeated the details of my uniform to me. I had, at long last, come home and been fully accepted in the Camp of Twenty-Six.'

Nogidela's speech

"I will school you with six duties, of which you sabela four and two complete The Number, a Glas for a Glas and a Draad for a Draad. Firstly, you remain at your post day and night; secondly, you look out for any danger threatening the camp; thirdly, you look for money with your 26 for the camp and its leaders; fourthly, you will use your skills to work yourself up to the post of Nogidela. I have six numbers on my blackboard. Salute! Numbers of men, money, drugs and goods, each under my single authority. Salute! Now I must take you and place you between myself and Sgt. Two, because I will school you with each and every number under my control and Sgt. Two will teach you to drill every six years. Salute! At ease! Attention! Salute!"

📖 note: it is the Nyanga (the respected and feared African doctor) who administers the oath; in the 28 Camp he also decides the new recruit's sexual status - Silver or Gold Line. *Umyango* is a doorway in Xhosa (entry point) and *sango* a gate – sangoma a traditional healer!

Pros and cons of status

Before a recruit goes to his initiation he is nothing but a despised *bandiet* in the prison. He comes from the Twelve Points feeling affirmed. Even the warders respect him. He has status, power, privileges, brothers to support him, a sense of importance, and identification and, more than that, he now has a role and a goal and something to fill the endless, boring hours of captivity. So what's wrong with all that? The problems arise and he may begin to reconsider his decision when he has to *maak vol Die Nommer*. By then it is far too late. He is no longer permitted to think for himself and will be severely punished if he declines to co-operate.

Special circumstances

In prison the gangs encountered special circumstances that defied the usual rules. They accommodated by introducing a series of *juries* that are made up of the seniors from the Twelve Points and these juries deal with special circumstances. A jury is defined in the dictionary as a body of persons (usually twelve) *sworn in to render a verdict or selected to award prizes or to try final issues of fact in civil or criminal cases and pronounce a verdict.*

Juries van Mameera/Papiere – restriction applied when a gang member is transferred to another prison and *awaits the arrival of his official papers.* The Number considers other prisons in the same way we would view another country and they are referred to as the far countries the *verre ilizwe* (*verre* from Afrikaans and *ilizwe* from Xhosa). He awaits his passport. I was told: "You sit under observation for six days, then you are called to answer to The Six (leadership) and this waiting is to find out if anything happened like rape or blood flowing (hit on head with a padlock) at the previous prison and you have not disclosed it and try to keep in the gang. Only then are you admitted (when purity of your position is established). Weakness is punished. Your name is on the slate or off the slate."

📖

The member must be observed, questioned and information on his circumstances compiled before he is awarded his usual status in the gang; if something happened to him at a previous prison – if he was raped, or he was waiting to be tried by his gang brothers and he was just absorbed into the gang without a full investigation this would reflect badly on The Number. He is expected to wait six, seven or eight days (termed years) depending on which gang he owes allegiance to. During this period the man is under observation and will be interviewed by *die Glas en Draad.*

Eventually he will be asked to define in detail the uniform he was given at initiation. Once the leadership is satisfied he is accepted back into the gang and accorded full status.

Juries van Volle Kantore – if a member is given promotion or moved to another prison and there is already someone with that rank then he must wait in The Mambozas (mbomboza: the dark of an approaching storm/trouble brewing) or The Forties (the roaring Forties) until needed; he becomes a sleeping partner and will assist with the schooling of other members. He may also be called on to take up office *vir die minute* or 'for the moment' if there is a temporary vacancy when the person who is accorded the position is ill, or goes to court or *agter die berge* (into solitary confinement). This rule prevents squabbles developing over who actually handles the job.

Juries van Skole – when the candidate is receiving tuition for promotion; schooling is usually given in a group unless a member is a candidate for a superior position and needs individual tuition.

Juries van Volle Nommer – awarded when the member has learned everything; the members are not given all the facts at once, for example: "There are seven six-point stars on the flag of 27, but later you are taught that these stars are also blood red and you are given the reasons. They don't give it all at once."

Juries van Condemned – if a member is injured and disabled and not able to perform his duties then he waits in the juries of the condemned until able to take up his full position.

Juries van Frontline/Sake – if a member is sent to the Frontline then he is expected to perform a gang duty (he is dutied), which usually means he must stab a warder. If the member is unable to do this then he himself will be stabbed, usually in the head.

Juries van Plase/Farms – is a place for the elderly inmate who can no longer perform gang duties. He will get everything on a platter. I was told: "You see, when Nongoloza and Ngilikityane went to Rabie's farm then the old farm workers were badly treated and some had been gored by the bull Rooiland. Rabie just let the old people rot." The implication being that The Number looks after its own.

protocol

Apart from this there are special rules regarding: how members of another gang can be addressed when on official business, the drilling procedures for soldiers, when a man is stabbed (Bomvana Slasluka) and when a brother dies. The latter is termed *short-arms*. The brothers mourn in silence with their hand held at chest height (almost on the heart) fingers indicating a salute, thumb touching the chest (for a 26). Nor may you ask another gang member, out of the blue, what his rank is; this can cause trouble: "You must always work through the lines of authority. Nongoloza (the 28s) never approaches danger first. The 27 investigates and then reports back to the 28s. This prevents chaos, stops anyone from just 'doing their thing'. When a new inmate enters a cell he stands at the toilet pot (neutral territory). The 27 must visit him first (spin the Number) and let the 28s know who the new addition is."

walcross

A period is set aside in the morning when the 28s hand over to *Mense van Sontop* (the 26s who work in the day) so that the three branches of The Number can communicate on issues affecting the prison gangs. (When the gangs meet it is always at the same crossroads where Ngilikityane and Nongoloza parted company and they act out the roles of the original gang leaders. In the story Nongoloza came back at dawn and he and Ngilikityane then questioned each other as to what they had each been up to.) This occurs at a special place named Walcross (frequently misinterpreted as *valcross* by those not fluent in Afrikaans). Literally translated the word is made up of *wall* plus *cross*. A figurative wall is constructed in the minds of the gangs *almost like a bridge*. To bridge the road a mud wall or rampart is constructed so that the leaders can have access to each other without actually standing on the crossroads, which is a symbolic dividing line. The issues discussed may be routine or murderous in intent. At this meeting *Die Glas* (Inspectors from each gang) *downs*, and is permitted to speak. The Captains from each gang act as watchdogs. *The Draad* (Wireless Operators) will act as the communication channel to report verbatim, back to his section, everything seen and heard and the conclusions reached: "*Die Draad*, he stands *pos* and he must have total recall because he reports back to the camp everything that has been said and by whom. He is full-force *geBritish* (well armed) and he does not *down*." My informant chuckles: "Just press play and *the Draad* is like a tape-recorder and he repeats everything that happened so you think you were there."

maak vol die nommer

The prison gang system is complex, sophisticated, entrenched and vicious. The power of the gang members must never be underestimated. It is a mistake to patronise the gangs as a group of superannuated boys engaging in a game of Cops and Robbers, Cowboys and Indians, Dungeons and Dragons, Play Station or Boer and Brit. It might appear as if there is something naïve and childlike about the way they have organised their fantasy: handing out roles, initiating members and donning invisible clothing. But it is *not* child's play. The Number plays-for-real and the new inmate steps straight into Golding's *Lord of the Flies* when he is ordered to *Maak vol die Nommer* with an act of violence.

human rights: the issues

It is nonsense to perpetuate the myth that the Number Gangs are romantic outlaws and it is a dangerous to delude oneself into believing their shabby stories about The Number having noble origins. History conclusively proves that The Number never, ever had any desire to assist the poor, never, ever intended to lobby – in anything but the most superficial and selfish manner – for better prison conditions, nor did The Number take a stand against the apartheid regime. It has never supported a political movement. The prison gangs were not part of the struggle and were despised by political prisoners who were held in separate sections of the prisons. The Number Gangs prey on the weak and focus on conducting their activities with as little interference from the authorities as possible.

The gang has a bloody history.

The Ninevites were marauding bandits who traversed the countryside from Natal, across the old Transvaal and as far as the Swazi border, advancing on towns, holding up farmers, killing policemen, hacking the flesh from living animals and leaving the beasts to die a gruesome death. Once in prison any resistance to the will of the gang was punished. Men who refused to become *wyfies* were strangled. There is evidence for this in judicial records. (van Onselen and the case of Matshayli Zungu)

The prison gangs remain as corrupt as the *apartheid* system they claim they opposed. The gangs should not be glamorised.

Since 1994 the prisons are no longer run on strict military lines, the warders no longer patrol the corridors with dogs: but the common prisoner's lot is no lighter, because gang rules are still brutally and rigorously enforced. The rapes and the fighting and the cell burnings continue into the New Millennium. Democracy brought an opening of South Africa's borders and increased drug trafficking was one result. The majority of prisoners abuse drugs. The prison gangs compete for the drug trade. For the Drug Lords it's about money and running their empires with impunity from behind prison walls.

It's about affluence for a privileged few.

New inmates are as vulnerable as they have ever been. They have little choice but to go along with the gangs. Anyone who interferes will find retribution to be swift and brutal.

It was never about human rights in the old South Africa, it is not about human rights in the New Democracy. Although some gang members will prattle on about politics and freedom and talk nostalgically about a lost purity, it must be understood that there is no place for human rights within the Number Gangs. There is nothing humane or just in the way the gangs operate. The senior judicial hierarchy in The Number will pass judgement on a disobedient gang member in his absence if they consider a serious offence has been committed – the man may have refused to carry out an order or given away gang secrets to the warders – the accused has no legal representation, he has no leave to appeal in his own right and the sentence will come as a most unwelcome surprise. He will be badly injured in a stabbing, possibly raped or even gang raped.

A 26, once raped, is ostracised and almost invisible to his ex-brothers and lives in constant fear of attack.

📖

human rights? no way!

There is no culture of human rights within the prison gangs and nothing emphasises this more than the punishment rituals, which are in total opposition to the South African Constitution. The Number has been quick to use the Constitution to strengthen the position of the gang as a whole, but the gangs show no willingness to work with the authorities to stop the rapes and the drug smuggling. The gangs operate, and probably have always done so, by trading in illegal commodities such as drugs and sex.

The Number codes are designed to allow very difficult personalities to coexist with a degree of harmony. The rules and threats of punishment act as the conscience of the gang. This sounds very positive, but unfortunately the rules and codes have been put in place to sustain a counter-culture to which members must submit without question to enable the The Number, not the individual, to thrive and survive intact.

It is The Number that they worship.

The new recruit truly understands the term *maak vol Die Nommer*, when he commits what his gang brothers have decided is an offence or omission. It could be something as minor as overlooking the accepted lines of communication and having gone above the next in command with a complaint. The direct translation is *fill up The Number* or *complete The Number*. In Zulu they say: *"Ndiyaze!"* In isiXhosa it's: *"Gcwalisa!"* in Afrikaans there is a hybrid-version: *"Vedala die Nommer!"*

It's used almost as a mantra by members of all three prison gangs. By implication — by punishing the disobedient The Number is purified and again operating at full strength.

At no point must any person's action be allowed to detract from the status of The Number, impinge on its power or discredit, defame or shame it. When this happens The Number decrees that some corrective action will take place so that the power and strength of The Number is not diminished but is reclaimed, thereby erasing any shadow over its name. It's this doctrine, instilled at initiation, that makes The Number so dangerous.

It is not uncommon for members to break the rules. After all, prisons are packed with miscreants. The fact that these men are drug addicted and also anti-social leads them into doing some pretty stupid things and thinking they can get away undetected. They steal from each other, take drugs on credit with no possibility of repaying, they negotiate with warders for personal gain and then there is envy — that too might lead to a man's downfall. Apart from this they must always be ready to carry out the work of the gang. Not being ready, or prepared to obey, is construed as gross insubordination.

When a man has been warned three times – depending on how seriously he has brought The Number into disrepute – he will be taken either to the Four Points or the Twelve Points.

The Number is now in a position to right a wrong and in the process some other member of the gang will more than likely rise in status.

In the gangs this is referred to as *masilon* or aggression — also spelled *massiljou* and *masilong* and *masilo*. It appears to have been taken from the word for *soldier* in the 28 Gang, which is *masjallou* or *amasoji*. It should not be confused with *carry on*. This is something initiated by warders when prisoners are aggressively disciplined by special units employed by Correctional Services.

In the 26 Gang when *masilon* is carried out the following occurs: "If a 26 do a small thing wrong, like saying you'll do something and not doing it, not keep your word, that could lead to a hitting. If the hitting happens nobody can see what's happening except the brothers. Three or four brothers close a corner with sheets and six brothers are inside the enclosure, including the brother that will be hit makes seven. The six brothers form a circle around the one that will be hit. He goes on his knees, fists on the ground and his head, should I say his face, must face the ground so that they won't hit the head because that is forbidden. There are also two brothers who give the orders to hit and to stop and they see that everything goes as procedure. You are not allowed to shout, stand up or lay on the ground if you are beaten on your back. If the two guys who monitor the procedure has a grudge, or don't like you, you get beaten for a long time. And that is painful 'cause you can't even lay on your back and if someone just touch your back you feel like you could scream a roof off a house."

The weapon could be bars of soap in a sock, but sometimes the victim is beaten with padlocks.

📖

A member may not refuse to go through with the procedure when gang punishment is handed out, nor can anyone else have any say: "No one may interfere in a sentencing. If you do then you and the victim share the same fate. *Die wat pos staan* must make sure the warder is not going to appear and halt proceedings. And you are always *lus vir werk*. If you are not ready to do the gang's bidding you pay with blood."

If the gang have marked a member they will carry out the duty assigned to them. The guilty party cannot escape — the orders to punish will follow the accused no matter what prison he is transferred to.

In this manner The Number demonstrates that it bestows power, but equally it can take all power away. There is no concern for the individual.

It's The Number that matters.

When the Four Points of the Silver Line in the 28 Gang meet to discuss an offence the Silvers One and Two and Goliaths One and Two are joined by the Landdros. The offender is called and the Silver Two reports on the offence. The Landdros decides on a suitable punishment and then leaves while it is meted out.

The Landdros then returns and pronounces: "*Vedala die Nommer, Salute!*" The offender is asked not to do it again, not to bring the number into disrepute. The number is cleansed and made complete by this ritual.

101

No one is above punishment, except that *wyfies* in the 28 Gang are punished as children: "They must blow the cheek up with air and then get a slap on the face."

When a private (wyfie) in the 28 Gang is accused of a serious offence then the Gold or Bloodline is responsible for his behaviour and blood is taken on his behalf while the private is *schooled* — which most likely implies a gang rape to teach him the error of his ways.

"The one who defends the private, then that person goes to *Juries van Sake* accompanied by the *Glas* and *Draad* who must see that the stabbing is properly executed. He is given a knife and must target either a warder or a non-gang member. Following the stabbing a second member must perform a similar deed but less violent, without blood running, so that he too can be sent *agter die berge* to the punishment cells, but for a shorter period, to be taught the work of the first accused so that his position will not lie vacant."

Of course, if the Gold Line member transgresses he *must* commit a stabbing to clear his name. In this manner The Number is made whole again and cleansed over and over again.

The inmate, in a flamboyant mood, was eager to continue my education: "We don't kill outright and we no longer use ground glass. We take a *bloukoppie* head (poisonous lizard) and dry it and grind it up and mix it in the man's food and get a private to sit with him and make *geselskap* (conversation) so the victim feels good and they chat until every bit has been eaten. Then the private is called and questioned closely as to whether he has carried out his duty and the man has eaten every morsel and then it's *you know nothing, you saw nothing!* "

Not totally plausible, more than likely another metaphor, but the knowledge employed – that this particular lizard's head is highly toxic – points to early gang knowledge gleaned when they still roamed the veld around old Johannesburg. These lizards, known as *bloukoppies* or *koggelmannetjies*, have a quaint habit of running, stopping suddenly in their tracks and then bobbing their heads up and down. They are not that common and particularly difficult to acquire inside prison compounds.

Previous researchers talk of men forced to admit to murders they did not commit, of soldiers taking their *wyfies* to the death chamber with them, of many gang related deaths. These days it is unusual for someone to be killed by the gang. The prison gangs must ensure a continuous supply of new recruits. Too many death sentences and there's no point in joining.

Between 1999 and 2001 there were 112 deaths following prison assaults – 46% were said to be gang related – indicating a decrease from the 1970s (1974 to 1978), when some 77 prisoners in the Western Cape *alone* were sentenced to death for murdering 41 fellow inmates in gang-related incidents. But even in the 1970s, when violent gang activity was assessed as exceptionally high, across *five prisons* in a period of *six years* only *one prison* showed over *ten gang related deaths*.

The average lifespan of a community streetgang member is probably far shorter than that of a prison gang member.

the venerated

Nongoloza, originator of the system, is revered by the 28 Gang. Ngilikityane (also called *Die Hollander* because of his aggression) is head of the 27 Gang and, because of the close connection between the Camp of 26 and 27, he is held in high esteem by the 26s along with the mysterious man named Grey; some members also refer to the former as Sir George Grey, an historical figure from the Colonial Era.

the invisible

Apart from their heroes Nongoloza, Ngilikityane and Grey, each of the Number Gangs has a *symbolic* head. But these posts are permanently vacant. These are celestial positions and there is enough information to indicate that the incumbent leaves his earthly life behind him shortly after his appointment!

📖

The Lord/Umkhosi (translates as Chief — but has *Godlike* overtones) is the symbolic head of the **Gold Line of the 28 Gang**, he wears the uniform of the ordinary soldier and he sits in the clouds stirring a three-legged pot full of blood. This Lord – he supposedly rose from a lowly rank of Second Sergeant – is considered a troublemaker the gang could not control. When the gangs fight amongst each other it is said: *The Lord kicked the pot of blood over.*

The Silver Line of the 28 Gang refer to the **Nozala in die Wolke** (parent in the clouds) whose *ngunya* (rank) is divided amongst officers in the line. He wears white with no insignia, as Silver Two 'he did not perform properly'. It is said that, along with The Lord, he is one of two people who stands half naked, half-way up the mountain. He is pointed out as a warning as to what can happen if you don't behave yourself!

103

The Lord of the Kapsale (Crossed Swords) sits at the **head of the 27s** with his personal pot of blood.

Makhwezi, with 16 *ngunyas*, has the last say in the **Camp of 26**. He is The Shooting Star.

I asked: "So Makhwezi, the Shooting Star, the symbolic head of the 26 Gang, is he alive, is he real, have you met him?"

My respondent frowned: "I think so. Or maybe Makhwezi is also Grey and died long ago." He threw some names at me, names of men whom he believed may have held this rank. But I had thrown him. The myth had seduced him into believing. If he were to be honest then he would admit that he had never met a Makhwezi.

There is much bloodletting on all ritual occasions in The Number. It would appear that they allocate these sinister posts to scapegoats in the gang, forcing them to take responsibility for prison murders if they cannot spare a valued ranking-officer.

Initiating a brother as *Makhwezi, Umkhosi, The Lord of the Crossed Swords, Parent in the Clouds* is a certain way to terminate their earthly existence.

In this way The Number sanctions human sacrifice!

finding ngilikityane – an authorial intervention

One of the most exciting experiences when researching The Number, apart from recording the *sabela*, was the apparent discovery of the real life Ngilikityane.

And it happened like this: a linking of serendipitous events that caused me to hold my breath, believing that I had indeed found the missing link in the chain.

I first saw Ngilikityane and Nongoloza in my dreams, *waking-dreams*, the kind that writers sometimes experience. I saw Nongoloza as a short, stocky man and indeed this is how he was described by his warders, although I only read their description much later. Ngilikityane came to me as tall and lean and ugly. None of his corners had been rubbed smooth, whereas Nongoloza was a real con-man, someone people warmed to, Ngilikityane handled all he encountered with brutality and violence and he frightened most men that he met.

Because Ngilikityane and Nongoloza existed I pondered for some time, asking myself the question: "Why is there so much information about this Nongoloza, but nothing more is ever heard of Ngilikityane?"

I asked my sources again and was informed that the gangs knew nothing about the demise of either man, *but that Ntolombom was an alternative name for Ngilikityane*. (It took ten years to find this out, ten years in which to ask the right question!) Ntolombom translates as The Arrow of Life or The Protector and even The Red Arrow (he did indeed protect the Sixes and the Codes of The Number by ensuring gang justice/law was honoured); an arrow has a head! Another word for head in isiXhosa is *ntloko* and *bomvu* is the isiXhosa word for red.

At this point I was also consulting the work of the historian Charles van Onselen and came across a description of the decline of The Ninevites: '*On the 16 December 1910 two prominent Ninevites – Chief George Schoko, alias Kleintje, and Jim Ntlokonkulu (Great Head) also called 'The Giant with the Crooked Eyes' – set out for work on the Main Reef Road in time-honoured fashion, assisted by two trusted Lieutenants. At about noon they intercepted three black miners making their way to Maraisburg, and immediately went into the abathelisi routine. Posing as detectives they first asked to see the workers' passes and then demanded their purses. When the workers refused to hand over their money, Schoko and his men assaulted them with sticks and overpowered them. They then relieved two of the workers of twenty-eight pounds worth of gold and administered a thrashing to the third who was unwise enough to be penniless. The Ninevites then returned to their 'fort' in the prospect holes near Canada Junction. The victims however made their way to the Langlaagte Police Station and reported the robbery to Detective Duffy and Constable King – the latter a veteran of the 1908 attack at the York Mine. Duffy and two of the miners set out towards Maraisburg in pursuit of the attackers, whilst King and the third worker searched the Canada Junction area. King had the misfortune to find what he was looking for. No sooner had he ordered the Ninevites out of their hiding place than he was attacked and fatally stabbed in the head. The terrified worker fled back to Langlaagte and reported the constable's murder. After a night-long search police eventually discovered King's body thrust into an ant-bear hole'.*

The brutal attack on a white official aroused widespread European indignation. On the night of 18 January 1911 the bandits were in the vicinity of Vlakfontein. Within forty hours of King's murder Jim Ntlokonkulu 'The Giant with the Crooked Eyes' was arrested.

When they sentenced Jim Ntlokonkulu to death later that year was it actually Ngilikityane who was sent to the gallows? I asked myself: "Is it possible that 'The Giant with the Crooked Eyes' could have been squinting because he shot his arrow at Nongoloza's stone?" Certainly he could not have used the title Khulu (Great) in prison as Nongoloza was the Nkosi Kakhulu in jail, but he would, like Nongoloza have used a prison alias and a different name outside jail. Was it possible that, in prison, it was Jim Ntlokonkulu (alias Ngilikityane) who became Ntolombom?

More questions followed: Was it more than coincidence that Ngilikityane was of Pondo or Xhosa extraction and that Jim Ntlokonkulu was of the same tribe? How likely was it that there were two generals in The Ninevites, a predominantly Zulu grouping, from the same Xhosa speaking tribe?

The evidence was compelling, but was it compelling enough?

Coincidentally, the day I started putting two and two together, I had a hideous dream, similar to the dreams I experienced when writing *The Prison Speaks*. In this dream, more an hallucination than a dream, a disfigured face, almost obscenely evil, imprinted itself on my mind's eye.

But my bubble burst when I consulted The Star newspaper for 26th April 1911. Jim Ntlokonkulu's given name was actually Jim Tanana. And his squint was real and had nothing to do with shooting arrows. In fact it was this horrendous squint that allowed the *terrified worker who fled back to Langlaagte* to identify Jim Tanana as the man who had murdered Constable King.

However, this does not mean that Tanana was not Ngilikityane. Perhaps another enthusiast will eventually uncover the truth, because the word for giant in Xhosa is not *ntlokonkulu* but rather *ingxamsholo* or *isigebenga*. This means his alias of Big Head was no reference to the man's physical appearance but had something to do with his qualities as a Big Chief!

Part Three
the world within

*It's a great drama — every member plays out his role in the story of
The Number in the course of the prison day.*

The mythology: the myths revolve around two issues — the legitimacy of
banditry and the origin and condoning of same-sex practices in an all male
environment.

The first book: this book was *'written'* when there was only one gang
with Nongoloza at its head — it was a *rules and regulations book* that
included information about ranks and roles, hierarchy, drilling, offences,
punishments. It's *the book* that tells them how to live and manage affairs on
a day-to-day basis.

Further editions: second and third editions of the story developed as The
Number split into two Camps and then three Camps. When the gangs were
arrested extra chapters were added describing the invisible uniforms of the
members and procedures to follow in extraordinary and unusual situations.

Their history book: the Phambuka Songaqo (The Crossroads), pronounced
Tambuka by Afrikaans speaking members who can't get their tongues
around an African language, is a deeply symbolic rendition of the history of
The Ninevites and was written after Nongoloza and Ngilikityane parted
company; it describes their origins and why two Camps were created and
the intricate relationship between the Camps. Later, some time after 1905,
the story of the formation of the Camp of 26 was added to the history book.

The homecoming: or The Long Road (or The Long and Winding Road) is
the first page of The Book that is taught to new recruits before initiation to
protect them from being absorbed into another gang. There are two main
versions. In the 28s' version all three divisions of the Camp of 28 are
referred to, but no mention is made of the 26s and 27s. The Homecoming
of the Camps of 26 and 27 includes the Camp of 28. The Homecoming
leads straight into the Initiation Ceremony.

Centre Post

Because the story tells them that Nongoloza worked in the prison kitchen to keep an eye on how the food was cooked, this area of the prison has become Centre Post for the Camp of 28. The majority of prisoners working in the kitchen area will be from this gang.

The Centre Post for the Camp of 27 is the prison exercise yard. They refer to the yard as *the spanga*, a place where they fight it out, sort out problems and, if the 27s have to stab another prisoner this is where it is likely to happen. To respect the territory of the 27s when in the exercise yard, and to acknowledge that they are now on 27 turf, the 28s will greet the 27s with "Hom! Hom!" They salute with three open fingers (not closed) and will then lower the middle finger so that they are actually saluting as 27. This only happens in the yard. In the cells the 28s salute the 27s with three closed fingers.

Chapter Eleven

 **Nongoloza's Book**

Nongoloza gave them a history, a military handbook and a code so that the gangs could live side-by-side with the minimum of conflict

introduction

The first litany that the novice is taught is The Homecoming also called The Long Road. More than one researcher has described the *sabela* as a litany, an intoned supplication with a biblical cadence and responses similar to a catechism. The Homecoming is linked to the doctrines propagated by the three branches of The Number. The law of the gang was said to be written on a stone — echoes of a clay tablet and the Ten Commandments!

man and myth: our shadow side

To ensure that his men never forgot his instructions, or the story of the gang, Nongoloza relied on the skills his ancestors used when he created his new mythology. Although Nongoloza could read and write, most of his men were illiterate, but those reared in a culture that relies on oral tradition have phenomenal memories.

A story is a narrative of imaginary or past events. A fairy story (about small imaginary beings) is similar to a folk-tale or even an urban myth. A fairy tale can also be interpreted as an incredible story or a falsehood. A myth is a traditional narrative usually involving supernatural or imaginary persons. A legend is also a myth, a story handed down from the past. There is a blurring of boundaries between these genres but, when one tries to classify the story that Nongoloza invented, mythology is probably the most accurate descriptive word. Fairy tales are told using a simple vocabulary and grammar. They also recount grotesque happenings in quite ordinary and everyday language. It's fascinating to note how Nongoloza, as the story-teller, follows all the traditional rules.

There is always more than one version of a folk-tale and, in similar vein, there is more than one version of Nongoloza's epic that relates the adventures and achievements of an anti-hero.

Each gang has adapted the telling in a manner that puts their chosen anti-hero in the best possible light.

To understand how Nongoloza manipulated the minds of his men one must understand that Zululand was, during his infancy and boyhood, a land in which legends lived. Every valley, hill and river had a story attached to it, stories involving spirits, ancestral animals and warrior kings. In their world spirits walked the earth and powerful, dangerous, phantom creatures inhabited the deep pools of the wide, African rivers. The tales that they heard in childhood were repeated around the campfires at night and it seems Nongoloza carried this tradition forward. It was not always possible to tell fact from fiction and, in the end, did it really matter?

Nongoloza's myth is set in the mine compounds and in an Africa conquered by the invaders. It is his life-story, thinly disguised, that he is telling. His story includes war and work, conflict with those in authority and the secrecy surrounding same-sex rituals. Zulu beliefs are combined with typical universal mythological conventions and symbols. It is a story rich in taboos and rules are broken at a price. In Nongoloza's story a man is murdered and his gall bladder cut from his body, an ox is sacrificed and the blood and gall is offered to Nongoloza and Ngilikityane to drink as a test — the dark side of the work of the witchdoctor.

Nongoloza possessed sufficient insight to know that he needed a narrator to tell his story, so he introduced himself in the third-person, allowing a character named Ngulugudu (or Pawule) to play the pivotal role. He relied on universal mythological symbols to penetrate the imaginations of his men, but simultaneously he included respected figures in African society, like the sangoma or wise man. There are witches and caves and seers and animals to be slaughtered and blood and body parts to be consumed in true African tradition. He used emotive imagery that reflected the kraals they recalled with affection. Despite the fact that many prisoners, particularly the Afrikaans speaking prisoners in the Western Cape, have never lived in a kraal or used the services of a sangoma, his story-telling skills were of such a nature that all prisoners revere the historical origins of The Number as gospel and believe Ngulugudu was a real person.

Fairy stories, myths and legends also reflect human truths — dark truths about man's shadow side that one normally prefers not to acknowledge. Even children's fairy stories are filled with shocking violence and cruelty. They have their own morality. Brother will trick brother to achieve a personal goal. Women abuse, abandon and murder innocent children while fathers turn a blind-eye, captivated by the sexuality of the new stepmother. In the original version of Sleeping Beauty the Princess Aurora was not awoken with a kiss by her prince charming. The sleeping virgin was repeatedly raped. Echoes of rohipnol and the first documented date rape!

The prison gang stories, like all good tales, rely on the willing suspension of disbelief (the fabulous and implausible), on repetition in the telling, so that the formula is not lost (very important to preserve an accurate oral tradition), the non-observance of logical time-sequences and usually the heroes have to answer a series of leading questions to qualify for the part they must play.

In the mythology of the prison gangs tasks are allocated, journeys of self-discovery and quests undertaken, wise men consulted, the ground opens and a mirror reveals the past and discloses the future, there are magic glasses (binoculars) that can see to the four corners of the earth, strangers appear on distant horizons, there is a sacred pure white stone (not a ring, but note the similarity), which is dropped and lost and comes into the possession of the disobedient *brother*.

The Number myth tells of *sibling* rivalry, severed heads on platters, human and animal sacrifices and the drinking of blood, secret potions and oaths spoken and mysterious objects buried with the dead. There are signs and portents, questions and responses, disembodied voices, gates waiting to be opened. Days become years. There is a pot of blood and falling stars, plus a damaged head — long before Harry Potter! And there is betrayal of the worst kind.

There are stories within stories and characters with more than one identity; plus invisible uniforms that only the initiated can see. There are echoes of the Brothers Grimm as figures appear carrying pitchforks and wearing blood-spattered garments.

There are words that protect and ultimately a man's position and safety within the gang structure depends entirely on how deep into the litany he can go, what he can recite. It's a battle of wits.

Was Nongoloza really the inventor of the myths or can they be attributed to Ngilikityane? Did the myths develop prior to the arrest of the Ninevites?

These are legitimate questions.

Nongoloza showed no reticence when he informed the prison authorities that the structure and hierarchy of the Ninevite Gang (almost identical across The Number spectrum) developed outside prison and that *he himself* modelled this gang on the British military and judicial system. He made, however, no mention of the mythological history or his role in its creation.

As a result there is only circumstantial evidence to indicate that the mythological history of the gang is of a similar age and origin — and that it developed outside prison and was invented by Nongoloza.

The basics of the oral history are identical in every prison and adhered to by all three gangs. If the story developed in a similar manner in all the prisons then we must presume they knew this story before they were arrested. If the stories had developed after the gangs moved into the prisons this would have proved an impossible feat as, when the Ninevites were arrested, they were sent to different prisons across the Transvaal and Natal.

When the gang split into two, some men going with Ngilikityane the others with Nongoloza, one can assume that they were already so steeped in the history and the management strategies of the gang that it made no sense to Ngilikityane to discard what worked well and invent something new. He kept the basic structure of a story invented to explain why such a tightly knit group had become two separate entities and just gave himself a more prominent role in the 27s' version. Significant changes might even have destroyed his credibility with his men.

A strong pointer to Nongoloza as the originator is the fact that the litanies are mostly in Zulu and Nongolaza was Zulu speaking. Even in the Western Cape the sabela relies more on Zulu and Afrikaans than on English or isiXhosa. The stories refer not to *kraals and huts*, but to *tents and camps* (of British military origin) with flags blowing in the wind and sentries at their posts wanting to know: *Who goes there?* These devices are used in the Homecoming of all three gangs.

Nongoloza made no bones about being infatuated with the British military as well as the British judiciary.

The litany of the 26 Gang confirms the order in which the three offshoots of The Number developed — first the 28 Gang, then the 27 Gang and finally *Die Manskap van Kroon* or the Gang of 26, while the initial page of the litany of the 28 Gang makes absolutely no reference to the later offshoots, which they surely would have done if the 28 Litany had developed in prison. There is also far too much similarity between the Book of 26 and the Book of 28 to be pure coincidence. It all points to a single point of origin.

There are too many parallels in the storyline to blame on chance.

A closer look at the available information indicates that Ngilikityane (impulsive, practical, unimaginative) valued Nongoloza's wisdom: he took with him Nongoloza's gang structure, rules, roles, values and punishment rituals. So why not pinch Nongoloza's version of the gang's history? Like many plagiarists it appears that Ngilikityane lifted what he wanted and modernised the litanies, putting his own imprint on Nongoloza's story, introducing the Xhosa word *isixhenxe* for the number seven and changing the name of Ngulugudu (the chief character in the story) to Pawule, a Pondo name, because his home language was isiXhosa.

Ngilikityane was clever, but not clever enough. He gave his own game away.

In the 26 version of the story Pawule, when he goes to the mines, meets an older man whom he greatly respects and this man assists him in inventing the language of fanigalore and in organising the other miners. Pawule calls this man Madala One. And, of course, Madala One, which means The First One, a respected elder, is just another one of Nongoloza's many pseudonyms!

The mythological history of Nongoloza recalls Hitler and the Nazi youth movement that developed in a disempowered Germany between the World Wars.

Youth of a defeated nation are impressionable. The men who joined Nongoloza were young, agile, strong and virile. Like Hitler, with his farcical rewriting of German mythology and the Aryan myth, Nongoloza developed a story to support and sustain his private vision.

The Zulu male was born to be a warrior and the white man took this dignity from him. Nongoloza would re-make them all warriors. He offered them back their manhood, status and power at a time when the battered Zulu image was looking for an heroic figure. Unfortunately, like the youth of Germany, the Ninevites got an evil genius!

1810, 1812, 1824, 1836

As the gangs tell it, a boat with settlers arrived in 1810 from Holland while the date 1812 signifies the beginning of The Number. This is the year in which, according to 26/27 history, a mythological figure from Pondoland called Pawule Mambazo (corrupted to Po or Paul) set off to investigate conditions in the mines and to enquire why the migrant workers did not return. The 28s refer, not to Pawule, but to a Zulu called Ngulugudu.

Although the gangs use different names for this mythical figure the meaning is the same: both Ngulugudu and Pawule mean *one who has been marked out* or *noticed* — possibly because of some notorious act or special attributes. (Of course the dates are fabricated. There were no mines in 1812 run by white men. The Great Trek had not yet happened.) The year of 1824 is the year that Nongoloza and Ngilikityane were made blood brothers by Pawule and saluted with the hand-sign of the 28s. The Year of 1836 is the year that, according to the story, the 26 Gang was inaugurated. The dates, giving The Number a much longer history, were possibly introduced to aid authenticity and add to their prestige. But there are some who are convinced that these dates are of a more recent origin and were introduced by the Afrikaans speaking prisoners in the Western Cape.

the crossroads

The *Phambuka Songaqo* (The Crossroads) is a record of historic events, partly fictionalised; it also enshrines the moral codes of The Number and is in a sense also their lesson book, a teaching tool and handbook for how particular issues should be dealt with and why. In isiXhosa *phambuka* means a crossing of the roads; in the Zulu tongue the meaning is more tantalizing, more convoluted — it indicates a deviation or a branching off, while *songa* is not only a winding road but implies disagreement and intrigue.

The Crossroads/Phambuka Songaqo (corrupted to *Tambuka* by Afrikaans speaking inmates unable to get their tongues around the more complex Xhosa with its final resounding 'q' – the palato-alveolar click!) is where Nongoloza and Ngilikityane fought over Magubaan and the issue of same-sex relationships and it is a point returned to time and time again in gang discussion.

Because the narrator fled from his home in Pondoland and into Natal the story takes place close to Greytown on the Mooi River which is a tributary of the Tugela River at whose source, incidentally, Nongoloza himself grew up.

In gang terminology *deep level* is synonymous with prison and throughout this myth the story is about the miner in his role as prisoner, because many prisoners were seconded as mine labourers. The arrival of Pawule at the mines reflects the arrival of the inmate who applies to join a prison gang. Simultaneously the narrator persuades his listeners that the reason for the subsequent behaviour of the characters in the story is justified because of the poor treatment men received in mines/prison and

114

we revisit the story of The Number coming into existence to improve conditions in prison. We also meet *Die Glas en Die Draad* (mine bosses) who later become two important figures in the gang hierarchy.

The listener is introduced to the shotgun ceremony which is used symbolically at the point where Pawule discovers his parents are dead and is repeated currently in gang initiation ceremonies when the recruit, in the presence of the Doctor or Nyanga must, by swearing an oath, acknowledge the gang as his only family. The colour white, as in *pure white stone*, is emphasised. This is the colour of the 26 flag. The word sixhenxe or seven and the introduction of Ngilikityane before Ngulugudu, tells us this is also The Crossroads of the Camp of 27. The words gall and poison (*gal en gif*) are synonymous with sex. And Delagoa Bay, the place that Nongoloza journeys towards, is the place where the sun does not rise, a reference to the night work of the Eights.

The stories are referred to over and over again, in the same way a minister of religion goes to his bible to illustrate a point or facilitate discussion; the stories act as a guide when the gang is in doubt and are used to settle disputes over moral issues. For example: Ngilikityane does not kill Nongoloza, he teaches him a lesson by injuring him. This indicates to the gangs that they must never wipe each other out because, in prison, they will always need each other.

Out on the street it's another matter!

style, semantics, devices

There are frequently repeated key-words such as *gcwala* (pronounced as in Zulu without the 'c' or dental click) which means 'to fill up' and *skangaka* (it may be a corruption of *kangaka* meaning 'this much/how many?' and indicates 'I am here or ready' or 'to be present' or 'to be there'). These repeated injunctions ensure that the listener is still following the story. There are also enigmatic coded slogans – *dissipline nommer* (this refers to the emphasis the gang places on the gang's work) and *salute* (this indicates something is well done or good) and a *jaar* (year) meaning a single day.

When Zulu or Xhosa words are used they may have several meanings and sometimes the meaning has been changed or the word corrupted because Afrikaans speaking inmates could not cope with the correct pronunciation: the Zulu word *phezulu* meaning 'heaven' or 'on top' is corrupted to *gebenzula or gephenzula* and implies to 'take up' and even 'steal' and *slasluka* which they sometimes use to mean 'work' or to warn that they are 'up to something/to maak vol Die Nommer' comes from the

115

Zulu *sahlukwana* - a verse of a hymn. There is also reference to *gevoleish* alternated with the word *gebruike* (from Afrikaans *gebruik* and meaning 'to use something'): a *'gebruike nommer one'* means dagga, *'gebruike two'* means cigarettes and *'three'* indicates food.

The origins of the words *tola* (hear) and *fotcha/focha* (see) were tricky to trace. In Xhosa the word *tola* can mean a diviner, a war doctor, one who can pierce deeply and *tolika* is an interpreter. Both indicate an ability to listen well. *Fotcha* possibly comes from the word *fotha* (Xhosa) for photograph – a visual image. Later it appears as if the word is altered to *fotsisa* (cause to see) and *fotsisana* (they saw) – meaning that they 'understood' the discussion.

Other words of interest: *phakamisa* (rise up, promote, propose) which they usually interpret correctly, but spell as *pakamiesa*; *dingena/dingela* comes from the Zulu *dinga* to require and is usually correctly used in context; as is *pikelela* from the Zulu *phikelela* which means 'continue obstinately, persist, persevere' but is also used to mean 'to take' and 'to go' or even 'go back' or 'went back' by the gangs; the word for 'give' is *nika* and they use this as *nikeza* meaning 'ask' as in 'asking to give information/ questioned/taking information from'; *chaza* (explain) which becomes *chaisana* and indicates a discussion and even 'do you hear me?'; they also rely a lot on the word *dala* which exists in both Xhosa and Zulu and can mean 'old, bring about, create, invent or institute' as well as *jigijela* or *jikijela* and this means 'throw' but they use it to mean 'to turn something around', whereas the correct word for 'turn about' in Xhosa is *jika*, however, on some occasions they use it idiomatically as when Pawule must *jikijela* or 'throw his eyes around/look all over'.

There are words such as *spanga* (do a job/crime – from Xhosa *isimanga*/astonish) and *gevoleish* and *baitela* which appear to be peculiar to The Number alone. *Kamandela* (catch out): probably an interpretation of *komondela* meaning *to commandeer*. *Stalala* has been translated as 'style myself'' or 'present myself as' because the dictionaries were of no help.

Or maybe I looked in all the wrong dictionaries!

I assumed that the pseudo-Afrikaans word *gevisinteer* which (for the gangs) means 'search' was adapted from the English word 'to visit'. Throughout the *sabela*, it's usually Afrikaans grammar that is imposed upon an African vocabulary.

A point of interest: Ngilikityane first introduces himself as *Skalaka* and not as Ngilikityane. He tells Pawule: *My stalala is Skalaka ek kom van Springs en ek is op pad myne toe om te spanga*. The word *skalaka* sounds a little like the Afrikaans word *skielik* and this name for Ngilikityane I was assured is not translatable and was: "Invented by the Coloureds." However, the word could be a corruption of the Zuku word *khalakatha* meaning 'swift entrance' or 'quickly' which sums Ngilikityane and his habits up very well indeed. This interpretation makes the use of the word *spanga* far more significant, it confirms that it is likely to be a corruption of the Xhosa word *isimanga* meaning 'astonish'. What fascinates is that Ngilikityane retains the Zulu word *isispohlongo* when referring to the number eight, but uses *isixhenxe* the Xhosa word for seven. The word *qamka* (pronounced without the click sound) is taken from Zulu *qkamuka* meaning 'to proceed from'. The word for the police/warders/bosses is given as *mapoeza* from the Zulu word for police: *phoyisa*. Farmer Rabie is referred to as a *mapoeza* to clue the listener in to the fact that he worked hand in glove with the mine bosses.

It is a story of revenge and retribution and it all starts in true story telling tradition with the words — a long time ago! It is only the first version, the story that the soldiers and sergeants learn. As men rise in rank they are taught more detailed versions of The Crossroads. For example - a more senior rank would include the information that: *while Pawule waited for seven years at the mine gates he was made to break up stones in the quarry* — which is, of course, exactly what vagrants were made to do to obtain passes in the old Transvaal.

The version learned by senior gang members will be embellished with little extras. For example: when Pawule/Paul Mambazo came from prison he carried with him the prison/mine keys with which he unlocked the doors to allow the prisoners/miners *to escape* and the prison book with the names of all the men. Key and book remain potent symbols in the Camp of 26. On a deeper level we are being told that the Story of the Number allows prisoners *to escape* into a world of absolute fantasy.

It must never be forgotten that no *frans* in prison may use sabela. When a prisoner speaks in sabela it indicates he has been given special information and the beliefs that go with that information, so that he has become a changed person. At the initiation it is the Fighting Generals who inform the new recruits of the laws of The Number, who give them permission to use the gang salute, to work on behalf of the gang and to speak the 'madodas' language', the language of the men of the prison gangs.

117

The Crossroads
Phambuka Songaqo - as recited by the 26s and 27s

Long, long ago, as far back as 1812, in a kraal in Pondoland, there lived, along with his parents, a wise man known to all and sundry as Pawule Mambazo. When Pawule's parents grew old and frail and were no longer able to support themselves, Pawule longed to turn the situation around for the better. *Gcwala!* Pay attention and just listen closely, because as Pawule dwelt on the problem he suddenly recalled that many times in the past *mapoeza van die myne* (mine gang bosses) had arrived at his kraal and selected people to go back and *slasluka* (work) in the mines on their behalf. *Gcwala!* Get an earful of this, strange to say, when these people of Pondoland returned from the mines there were many of their number missing and the wives of the missing men cried out and wept tears in their misery. *Gcwala!* Because of this whole sorry business, the people of the kraal got together and seeing as Pawule, a man known for his cleverness, had already made up his mind to go to the mines on his own, they asked him to go right in and look all over the mines to find out the truth regarding the whereabouts of the men of Pondoland who never followed the road back home.

Pawule Mambazo was most determined and he set out for the mines and at the gates of the mine *skangaka* he got into a discussion with two mine bosses who were guarding the gates, the one with a pair of binoculars and the other with a walkie-talkie radio. (Glas and Draad) And these bosses questioned Pawule most closely as to where he was going, who he was and what he was looking for.

Promptly he replied: *I am Pawule Mambazo and I am looking for work.*

The one boss with the walkie-talkie made contact with those inside the mine *en hy het die nommer gespeel* (note the layers in the story and the convolution because these men are searching to add to the strength of The Number which does not yet exist!) and told them all about this newcomer, Pawule, who was looking for a job.

To test Pawule Mambazo as to his true intentions they left him outside the gates of that mine for a full seven years. When the seven years had elapsed the *mapoeza* fetched Pawule and took him right inside the very mine itself. Then, to be sure he had the strength to survive the intense heat deep in the bowels of the earth, the *mapoeza* shut Pawule in a cave where they alone could control the temperature and test his strength. When they found him fit for work they immediately issued him with a pair of brown boots, khaki overalls, khaki helmet with a light attached, a pick and a spade and a sieve.

They cautioned him: *With this you will dig and sift and be sure to bring die wat salute het (the good stuff) to us each and every time.* And Pawule persevered even in the very depths of that part of the mine that was called the deep level.

And as Pawule worked there, deep inside the mine, he met other men speaking many different languages which meant that they could not understand each other, although they had been working together for a very long time. But Pawule was wise and he also encountered a respected elder, a man everyone recognised as Madala One, an old-timer who had been there even longer than the others. And, as the two of them discussed the business of the missing men that had brought Pawule there to the mines, Pawule and Madala One reached an agreement to take all the languages and turn them into one language that they called fanigalore, so that all the men in the mines could speak the same tongue.

At that very moment, *die jarre en minute,* that everyone was able to understand each other, they conversed earnestly about those who had died in the mines without receiving any help or support from the *mapoeza.* And Pawule asked many questions about those *witbene,* the dead men, who had never followed the road back to Pondoland. And Pawule got together with Madala One and they plotted together with the men of other nations to rise up against the *mapoeza* and take the gates.

Daar was jarred gesny, the years went by, and Pawule worked himself up until he held a trusted position in the offices at the mine and soon he could give an account of everything that happened, and had happened, in the mine. And in a jiffy, *die nommer daleka,* they did what had to be done and every single one of them took up what they needed to strengthen themselves. They grabbed money and gold as well as the book with the names of all the men who had died in the mines. Then it was time for Pawule to stop talking and he bolted for freedom.

The mine bosses gave chase with their dogs when the men broke free and some were killed, but Pawule escaped back to Pondoland to his kraal. Sadly he was far too late to be of help to his family, his parents had vanished. Pawule went to consult another wise man of the kraal who was called a seer, a man who saw visions. This man told Pawule his parents were dead. He opened the earth for Pawule with a one-time shotgun and showed him in a mirror the bones of his parents and then he demonstrated to Pawule how to offer respect, to take leave forever of his parents and to bring the whole business to a decent close with a two-time shotgun. When they were finished the wise man warned Pawule to flee Pondoland because the mine

119

bosses were hot on his heels and, because of all he had accomplished in the mines, they would certainly kill him if they caught him.

Pawule said his goodbyes to all he knew in Pondoland and fled into the mountains. On his journey through the mountains he discovered a kloof and, in exploring this kloof, he found a cave — an ideal hiding place. And it was in this cave, which Pawule would occupy for many long years, that he organised himself *in dissipline te sit*. When he had finished with this business (of robbing anyone who came his way) he gathered together and locked away in a safe place everything he might need (all the stolen goods) to strengthen himself and went to sit on a pure white stone at the entrance to the cave. Then he lit his pipe and enjoyed a good smoke.

Now Pawule had with him a pair of glasses (binoculars) that allowed him to look to the four corners of the earth. And this you must know, as he looked around, in his sights he could see a farm where a boss named Rabie resided with his Queen, and he could also see many beasts including, and you must remember this, a beast, a bull in fact, that had gored to death many men who had broken the laws of Rabie.

And after he had made himself comfortable with good food and a drink and a smoke and was once again ready on that pure white stone and studying the four corners of the world, Pawule became aware of a cloud of dust on the horizon. And this cloud of dust approached and came nearer and nearer to Pawule on his stone.

Pawule, who remained seated on his pure white stone, called out: *Stop! Who are you, where do you come from and where are you heading?*

A voice replied, boasting: *I call myself Skalaka, I'm a rascal from Springs, my style is to astonish all with the swiftness of my entrance and I am on my way to the mines for a bit of skulduggery.(Direct translation minus the nuance indicated by the words skalaka and spanga: I am Skalaka/Ngilikityane from Springs and I am on my way to the mines to get work.)*

Then Pawule Mambazo showed him: *I am that Paul Mambazo who came from Pondoland and you'd better get your head around the fact that I've been to the mines before you and anything worth taking has already been stolen when the gates were rushed. If you've got the guts to join with me in what I do then I can raise you up to be my right-hand man and the two of us can share everything we steal.*

Ngilikityane, for it was indeed he, examined the goods that Pawule had hidden away and he was impressed with what Pawule showed him and he agreed to join Pawule.

Then Pawule, because he did not quite trust this newcomer, searched Ngilikityane and removed the blade he carried. Then he took him right into the cave and showed him where he could sleep (he shared his turf with him) and they ate a meal together.

After making themselves comfortable they slept and woke with the first rays of the sun *en die dissipline vol gaan maak* (they went to rob others) on the banks of the river that is called the Mooi River. When they had finished they returned for a time to their cave. And so the years went by, until the day arrived when Pawule was once again *skangaka* (on guard) on that same pure white stone and he saw a second dust cloud in the distance.

Again Pawule called out: *Halt! Who goes there? Who are you and what do you want?*

A man replied: *I am Nongoloza. I come from Delagoa Bay and I am on my way to the mines.*

Pawule replied: *I am Paul Mambazo, I come from Pondoland. I've already been to the mines and taken all that was worth taking because the ways of the mine bosses are not just. Clearly we are two of a kind. I propose that you stand guard at my right-hand side and have a share in everything.*

When Nongoloza saw the goods that Pawule had put together he agreed to join him, and that Pawule, well, he told Nongoloza all that he had been busy with over the years and what went down at the mine.(In other words he shared something more with Nongoloza than he shared with Ngilikityane.)

Many years went by and Pawule decided that it was time to test the strength and loyalty of Ngilikityane and Nongoloza. It was time to send them to the farm named Leiland, that was owned by the farmer known as Rabie.

And it was in the seventh year that Pawule sent Ngilikityane and Nongoloza to the farm of Rabie to kill that bull that was there and to return to him with the bull's horns and blood and also with the gall bladder of the *mapoeza* (Rabie). Pawule told them: *You will know that bull because it wears a ring in its nose and has holes in its ears and scars on its face and is kept alone in a kraal of its own.* He armed them with bayonets and sent them to do his bidding. And Nongoloza and Ngilikityane when they arrived at the farm, did as was required of them and they killed Rabie and cut out his gall bladder. Then they killed the bull also and took the bull's blood and its horns. At this point Nongoloza did his own thing and he skinned the bull of Rabie. Ngilikityane tried to stop Nongoloza and reminded him: *Leave the skin, don't take the skin, Pawule gave no instructions and spoke no word about the skin of Rooiland the bull of Rabie.*

But Nongoloza took the skin and replied knowingly: *This skin will strengthen me now and in the years to come.*

Their business finished they both returned to Pawule at the cave and Nongoloza, on being questioned by Pawule about taking the skin of Rooiland, gave the same reply as he had given to Ngilikityane: *This skin will strengthen me now and in the years to come.*

Then Pawule took the blood and gall and mixed it in the horn of the bull Rooiland and offered it to Ngilikityane.

Ngilikityane took the horn and tasted, and spat the mixture out saying: *The blood salutes but not the gall! The blood is good, but the gall is not good.*

But as for Nongoloza he tasted and then swallowed the lot in one gulp and exclaimed: *Gonqo!*

Then that selfsame moment Pawule knew for certain which of the two men would follow his own desires. And he took their arms and cut their wrists at the pulse and made Nongoloza and Ngilikityane blood brothers forever. At the same time he warned them: *Never repeat the cutting of pulses and the sharing of blood. It will frighten others away. In the years that lie ahead you will encounter other men who will be strong enough to stand together with you and continue with the work you have begun. Their blood must not run. Instead, open their eyes with the one-time shotgun and the two-time shotgun.*

And it was in the year 1824 that Nongoloza and Ngilikityane were made blood brothers by Pawule. And in that year both of them, for the moment, saluted with *mzukwana-spohlonga*, the sign of an Eight! (the salute given in the world outside)

As time went on Pawule grew old and weak, but Pawule, who had left his kraal to go to the mines, he had the ability to see into the future and everything that he had seen from the beginning had come to pass and he knew he was at death's door. And for that very reason Pawule schooled Ngilikityane and Nongoloza in all that he knew (of the Number) that he had kept in his head and he shared his *special* thoughts with them. And he told them: *If it should happen that I am not here when you have finished the day's work, you will find me again beyond the mountains of Kahlumbe near Pietermaritzburg.* (In prison jargon 'behind the mountains' is a metaphor for solitary confinement.)

Time passed and men returned to work in the mines and Ngilikityane and Nongoloza robbed these men quite violently and took all that they wanted from them, for the work that Ngilikityane and Nongoloza were ordained to do was the work of *roof en plunder.*

Now it came about that one day when they returned after work they noticed that things had been removed from the cave in which they stayed.

It came to a point where it was decided that Nongoloza would work at night and Ngilikityane by day, so that there would always be someone at the cave to guard their spoils.

And Ngilikityane said to Nongoloza: *If I work in the day you will stand guard die slasluka wat skangaka is and, if you work at night, I will stand guard over the stolen goods, the fruit of our hard work.*

And they both got on with the business in hand and Nongoloza, on his way to and from work, met many promising, like-minded young men, not yet in a gang, who had the courage to join him in his work of *roof en plunder.* And Ngilikityane likewise, on his way to the mines, fell into discussion with many clever *franse* who were more than willing to join up with him so that, over the years, the two groups increased in number.

Now one day, when Ngilikityane came back from work, he found Nongoloza in the company of a boy, a *frans*, who went by the name of Magubaan. Then Nongoloza explained where the youngster came from and he and Ngilikityane shared food together. When they had eaten they said their farewells and Nongoloza went off to work. On his return, as the first rays of the sun breached the horizon, Ngilikityane was already on his way to meet Nongoloza at the crossroads and there, as usual, they discussed business and Nongoloza showed him what he had acquired in a night's work and then they parted. But, that very same day, while Ngilikityane was hard at work, he received news that Pawule had indeed died beyond the mountains of Kahlumbe. Ngilikityane returned to the cave early to report the death of Pawule only to find Magubaan sleeping under Nongoloza's blanket. (In another version Magubaan stays at the cave to look after Nongoloza who is supposedly ill.)

Ngilikityane demanded of Magubaan: *Why aren't you also at work?*

Magubaan replied: *Nongoloza told me that I cannot do two jobs at once.*

In surprise Ngilikityane asked: *What is this other work that you do?*

Magubaan replied cheekily and showed Ngilikityane: *Knock the stone three times and the water flows and you can go and ask Nongoloza yourself.* (A metaphor for sexual activity that makes men sweat.)

Nongoloza was *bymekaar met 'n dissipline nommer*, that is to say he was busy on a job (robbery), when he heard Ngilikityane's bugle summoning him to a meeting. Nongoloza armed himself with a knife and headed for the crossroads. Firstly Ngilikityane greeted Nongoloza with the Salute of Eight. He told him of Pawule's death and questioned him about Magubaan. Nongoloza shrugged it off as before: *The youth will strengthen me now and in the years to come. You can see what he's good for just by looking at him.* Then Ngilikityane confronted him and declared that Pawule had never taught them to do what Nongoloza had done. Ngilikityane reached for his weapon at his left side and he stabbed Nongoloza.

Nongoloza asked: *If you kill me who will continue our work?* Ngilikityane replied: *I do not want to wipe you out, only the wrongs that you do.*

Then Nongoloza turned and fled across the green veld and the blood flowed from him and formed a thick red line across the countryside and there appeared the living Flag of 28.

Then the heavens and earth split asunder and a star fell from the sky and landed right on Magubaan's forehead. In addition Ngilikityane stabbed Magubaan so that, for ever after, he would recognise Magubaan and the scar from his wound would be eternal proof. (The falling star/shooting star is a metaphor for Ngilikityane. Magubaan of the Camp 28 carries the imprint of a star on his forehead. This implies that Ngilikityane came down really hard on Magubaan!)

Then Ngilikityane and Nongoloza discussed together that they would have to bury the bones of Pawule and study and learn from those same bones. But first Nongoloza's wounds were attended to and only then did they set out to bury the bones of Pawule in the mountains named Kahlumbe — a quiet place, a good place to sit in silence when one is muddled in thought and needing answers. Ngilikityane was right there and ready with a piece of bark covered in writing. He took that bark and he buried it in Pawule's grave.

When they had finished burying Pawule the two men parted company and Nongoloza returned to Delagoa Bay and Ngilikityane went in the direction of Springs. Before they went their separate ways Ngilikityane showed Nongoloza that he would no longer swear an oath with three fingers, as an Eight, but he would take one finger away.

Ngilikityane told Nongoloza: *From this day forth you will know me by the Sign of Seven.*

📖

The 28s' version of The Crossroads is rather different. They claim that it was Ngilikityane who sent Magubaan to Nongoloza and that the two men subsequently fought over possession of Magubaan (and that this is *the secret* – because Magubaan is not in the Camp of 28) and that it was the Wiseman (Pawule/Ngulugudu) who said: "If you injure each other who will carry out my work?" The 28s argue that the laws were written on the pure white stone and wrapped in Rooiland's skin which Ngilikityane dropped (careless of him!) into the Moliva River (not on modern maps, but most likely the Mooi Rivier) and as the stone rolled down the bank it hit a tree and broke in half and only a portion of the rules were imprinted on the bark which Ngilikityane removed (and possibly buried in Pawule's grave); but Nongoloza sent Magubaan to fetch the stone from the river and he came out covered in droplets of shining, silver water and this gave them the name Silver Line as well as the complete set of rules which condoned same sex activity. According to the 26s Magubaan only retrieved half the stone so the 28s do not have all the rules of Pawule either. But the 28s counter this by explaining that the stone had been wrapped in the skin of Rooiland and a perfect imprint was made on the skin (*the skin that would strengthen Nongoloza in the years to come*) of the *complete book of* rules. This helps Nongoloza to justify continuing his same-sex practices. Either way, he claims, they have *all* the rules of Pawule.

What is obvious is that, with the burying of Ngilikityane's version of the rules in the grave with Pawule, clarity on the ethicality of same-sex practices in an all-male environment is never going to be reached. And, in the end, we do not know what Pawule thought about this matter as, in yet another version, Ngilikityane asks Pawule outright about the correctness of same-sex activity and Pawule declines to answer him but instead tells Ngilikityane to go to the mines and see for himself. (A bit odd as Pawule had already been there, so he could, if he'd wanted to be less obscure, have given a direct answer.) Ngilikityane proceeds to obey orders and when he gets back discovers Pawule is dead. There is no record of what Ngilikityane saw in the mines.

Naturally there is much dispute about the red line on the flag of 28. The 28s claim it is the blood of the slaughtered beast Rooiland.

In the 28s rather bloodier version of The Crossroads the two men returned to Pawule with the head of Rabie. The blood they drank was their own blood when their pulses were cut and neither Ngilikityane nor Nongoloza could stomach the blood or the gall of Rabie. According to the 28s' version Ngulugudu (the 28s name for Pawule) said: *Your blood is not sweet for each other.* But both versions concur that Pawule expressly forbade them ever to repeat the blood brother oath and since that date it has indeed been replaced with the shotgun ceremony.

Delagoa Bay is on the coast, at the time it was Portuguese territory and had existed for some time, but the mention of South African place names, such as the mining-towns of Springs and Germiston, in Nongoloza's Book, gives us some indication of when the story was invented. Springs, a colliery centre on the East Rand came into existence in the 1890s, but Germiston, named after a place near Glasgow in Scotland, was already established by 1887.

From this we can determine that the split between the two men occurred at some point in the 1890s.

Now the road to Springs from Johannesburg is called the Main Reef Road and it bypasses Maraisburg, Langlaagte and Canada Junction – all names connected with the mysterious Jim Tanana, the Big Chief, the *Giant with the Crooked Eyes* who, in 1911, hotfooted it down the Golden Highway only to be arrested at Vlakfontein and executed in prison.

halt! who goes there?

When a young man goes to prison for the first time he is going, at some point, to be intimidated by gang members who will try their luck with him and nudge him and enquire: *Wie's jy by die tronk?* (Who do you think you are in this prison?) He will already have been fed the fearful stories of rape and dagga pokes. He may have watched while another prisoner was victimised. It might seem a good move to join a gang so that the second time he is pushed around he will be able to reply with some *sabela* which will identify to which gang he owes his allegiance. When an inmate indicates interest and shows some promise, he will be taught a few pages from The Book, from that part called The Homecoming and up until where the new inmate meets, in the case of the 26s, the man called Nogidela, the tutor of the soldiers in the Camp of 26. If an inmate can recite these pages then he is protected and another gang cannot initiate him.

What follows is a comparison of the first pages that are given to members of the 26 Gang and 28 Gang to protect them prior to initiation. There are many similarities between the two litanies.

Both gangs use the word *frans* for an innocent prisoner, both characters are looking for work (a metaphor for deciding which gang to join), both characters live in the bush (a metaphor for the prison where uninitiated prisoners live), both characters are met and challenged by a sentry and have

126

to decide which camp to join, both refer to the Crossroads (kruispad). The 26 Gang litany indicates that the man is already in prison and alone, the 28 Gang litany indicates that the character has only just left the parental home. And the litany of 28 mirrors most closely the life-experiences of Nongoloza. The pages from the 26 Gang litany, because they were workshopped in prison, indicate that the man has a choice; he can join any of the three gangs. The 28 Gang litany, because it is the oldest and was possibly learned before the gangs were entrenched in the prisons, makes no direct reference to the Camp of 27 or 26 other than to refer to sunrise and sunset (the two are metaphors for the fact that Nongoloza worked by night and Ngilikityane by day). The 28 litany refers to the pure white stone and includes many symbolic references to the same-sex practices of the Camp of 28, including the word *left* which indicates the female line. The new recruit, in the 28 Homecoming, is asked to choose between a weapon (khanda-khanda) and a penis (banana), if he chooses the latter, because he is preordained to join the Silver or Female Line, he sneezes twice; the Gold Line recruits take up the weapon and sneeze once or three times.

The ritual of taking snuff is important in sangoma divination in African culture and sangomas carry on their person a bull's horn containing snuff that they offer to the spirit world. The word kanna-kanna/khanda-khanda in the following text is used to indicate a hot headed person and is a symbol for a weapon or violence (which the *wyfie* avoids) and comes from the Hindustani word khábá for highly spiced food (*khanda* is head and also the head of a penis in Zulu). The Silver Line recruit must refuse the curry but eat the banana, because he is destined for a soft life in prison!

How, I asked myself, did a banana ever manage to make such an incongruous appearance in this solemn undertaking? Then I discovered that the Zulu word for desire and concupiscence is *khanana*. Could this be another corruption, by those speaking Afrikaans as a home language, of the original word? Khanana to banana! It's a fair question.

Because there are three divisions in the Camp of 28 there are three slightly different versions of the Homecoming of the 28s. The three versions reflect the work of the Silver Line or The Twos, consisting of the *wyfies* or *seuns* (boys) as they prefer to be named, and the two branches of the Gold Line (Bloodline) whose role is to defend the Camp. The Gold Line consists of the military wing, referred to as The Ones and the Third Division which includes the fighting soldiers of the Camp of 28.

In the Camp of 28 the older members, when discussing the Homecoming, are more likely to use the original Zulu words and refer to the *umzakwaan* (the place outside prison from which the new intake of prisoners comes) which the initiate must forget all about. In accordance with African tradition they do not like, out of respect, ever to refer directly to titles or names such as Nozala (parental figure) or even Magubaan or the oath. These names are implied in the litany of 28 and in the same manner, in the Homecoming of the Camp of 26, the flags that the *frans* sees are described, but there is no mention of 28, 27 or 26 (the numbers are implied.) This could be convention or it possibly indicates that, when these litanies were originally learned, the gang was not known as The Number.

The Glas, for all the Camps, resides in the 'bush' to spy on the new recruits. New recruits must learn the meaning of the litany by constantly referring to their teacher – Sergeant One or Nogidela if a 26. It's the teacher who escorts the new recruit to the initiation.

Each line of the 28 Camp will react differently at points in the litany, depending on whether the Doctor has decided their heart beats once (Gold), twice (Silver) or thrice (for the Gold Line soldiers). It must be remembered that they do not have free choice as to which line they will enter as this is decided prior to initiation and confirmed by the Nyangi (doctor) who examines the new recruits.

Throughout, the symbolism of *left* and *right* is vital, and the left line, the Silver Line, must down (kneel on the left knee with the right knee up/this is reversed for the Gold Line) with arms folded. It is said that the one who chooses light work cannot ever touch the assegai (the knife that killed Rooiland); and each line may only sabela with members of the same line, in other words, with their own *manskap van chaila*.

The Gold Line member will respond to the first voice and, when offered a choice, he will take up the assegai and he will be *dutied,* meaning that he will then be told to stab so that his rank will be vasgebrand, burnt into him.

The rules governing the Camp of 28 are far more complicated than those that apply to the Camps of 26 and 27 because of 'the secret' that alludes to same-sex practices.

📖

The first time I listened to a 28 gang member sabela was in Claremont in 1995. Dusk was falling and I had parked in the old parking lot behind the OK Bazaars. Earlier in the day I had assisted a young, handsome reprobate in court. He was unable to provide a fixed address and when the magistrate threatened to make him await trial in prison, I took a calculated risk and stood surety. He asked what he could do to repay me and I asked for a page from *The Book of 28*.

He obliged.

In reciting the extract his whole demeanour altered. He retreated into a weird, enticing 'other' world, one about which I knew very little. He began with a role-play, a question and response routine that resembled a catechism. From his recitation I concluded that he had begun his prison time as a wyfie in the Silver Line of the Camp of 28.

📖

"Chaisana gwala gefortcha, hoe sal ek wys raak?" he asked. *(How can I acquire the knowledge.)*

Then he changed persona from supplicant to catechist: "Wie is djy wat soek?"

"Hoe sal ek rerig wys raak, ek is die stem wat soek?" *(I am a voice that truly seeks the knowledge that will make me wise.)*

The catechist: "Gwala Nongoloza!" *(Acknowledge Nongoloza!)*

📖

He continued without taking a breath and I wrote like fury. He recited the story of an young innocent man who leaves his parental home to find a job. He comes to a forest and waits for a year until all his rough edges have been smoothed away. He makes his way to the crossroads (Phambuka Songaqo) and after he has wiped the dust from his eyes and the dirt from his clothes he hears a voice. The voice summons him, but thinking the man is swearing at his parents he ignores the voice. The voice calls a second time and the youngster answers to the call of *Way, Way!* (Magubaan). A man, attired in uniform, comes up behind him and takes him by the left side/shoulder. The man (Sgt. Two of the Gold Line) wears khaki and carries a haversack. He wears blood red boots with white laces and his gold belt buckle is in the form of a lion's profile. The man in uniform accosts the youngster and asks who he is and what he is looking for. He replies that he is an innocent newcomer and looking for a job. The man in uniform asks him if he'd like to meet some men with scarred faces, rings in their noses and holes in their ears. (A pretty good description of the appearance of the bull with the scarred face (Rooiland) and a clear reference to the fighting men of the Gold Line.) He agrees, as long as they neither kill him nor chase him away. He is invited, if he believes he has the courage, to place his hand on the man's left upper-arm/side. (Left is synonymous with light, female work.) He accepts the invite to be a *wyfie and clasps the man's upper left*

129

arm/side. When the man in uniform asks him what he sees when the sun rises, he replies that he sees nothing at all. Next he is asked what he can see when the sun sets and he replies that he can see as far as a green tree (the guava tree with its soft fruit of which the pampered Silver Line must eat) and two stones/peaks. When he arrives at the tree he realises it is the men's resting place. He sits himself down on a red stone (stone of the Bloodline) and slips off, then he sits on a pure white stone (pure white stone of Pawule/Ngulugudu with the laws that, according the 28s, condone same-sex practice) – and remains seated. The man in uniform opens his haversack and takes out a cloth in the colours of the Flag of 28 — grass green, pure white and blood red. He places a weapon on red (the assegai/weapon that killed Rooiland), a banana on white and some snuff on green. (Snuff plays an important part in African tribal rituals.) He asks the newcomer if he can take up the weapon. Instead the youngster eats the banana (which tastes just right – a bit like Goldilocks and the Three Bears!) and takes some snuff and sneezes twice. (He rejects the kanna-kanna/kanda-kanda but eats the banana, takes snuff and sneezes twice thus indicating his allegiance to the Silver Line). Then the man in uniform packs all his paraphernalia back in his haversack and asks again what the newcomer can see at sunrise. Again the youngster answers that he can see nothing. (Sunrise indicating the Camp of 26/27.) He asks what he sees when the sun sets and he replies that he can see as far as a dark cave where people are speaking in a tongue he does not understand (the gang sabela).

📖

In 2005, and again in 2009, I was able, when working with two much older members of the Camp of 28, to confirm that the information was accurate. These men, long past their initiation date, knew the details of the story but were not able to repeat it any longer at top speed. They had forgotten the recitation!

The tree previously referred to is indeed a guava tree, full of soft fruit, easy for the wyfies to eat! They also corroborated that those who sneezed twice *slaan vir die werk van twees* in other words they would enter the Silver Line and not the Gold Line.

One of the men referred to the kanda-kanda as curry that was too strong for his taste (symbolic of a weapon). He said he told his sergeant *my bene sal vedala soes die jare sal kom en gaan.* In other words he did not have the courage to be a man of violence, to always fight for the Camp of 28 for the rest of his stay in prison, but preferred a softer life and so the banana was sweet to his taste. Gold Line members accept the kanda-kanda and find the banana too bitter (the Ones) or too sweet (the Threes) and they sneeze either once or three times. Finally it is explained to the new recruit that the mountain peaks are really his mother and father, the Lord of the Gold Line and the Mamzala (or Nozala) of the Silver Line.

After leaving the cave the new recruit is taken to a pure white building with a red roof and green window frames (all in the colours of the flag of 28), outside stands a silver flag pole with a flag waving in the wind. The flag is black, red, green and white. He is taken to the gates inscribed with a silver 2 and a golden 8. He enters the 'gates of no return' and goes to his swearing in ceremony which follows a similar pattern to the initiation ceremony conducted by the Camp of 26.

He has now reached the end of the Long Road of the Camp of 28.

Nongoloza's Voice
The Homecoming - the first page of the Book of 28

Jare terug was ek 'n frans toe ek my ma en pa gewys ek gat 'n werk soek. Ek het nie vir hulle gesê watter soort werk ek gat soek. Ek het geloop tot binne in 'n grasgroen bos, daar het ek gesitte vir 'n jaar. Die tweede jaar het ek uitgerol ronde klip, sonder hoek of kant. Ek het gerol tot op 'n kruispad. Ek het opgestaan. Ek het die stof uit my oë en my klere uitgevee. I walked and I heard a voice, "Way-way (umsunukonyoko!)" Ek het gedink hy vloek my ma uit, so ek het nie die stem gehoor nie. En ek het weer 'n stem gehoor: "Way-way (Magubaan!)" So ek het stil gestaan, ek het 'n hand op my linkerskouer gevoel, ek het omgedraai. Ek het 'n man gesien met 'n khaki uniform, khaki hawersak (Sergeant Two or Die Hawersak) and bloedrooi boots, met spierwit vetters, silver caspir met 'n goue halweleeu kop (lion head in profile). Hy het my gevra: "Who are you and what do you seek?" Ek het hom gesê: "Ek is 'n frans en ek soek werk." En hy het my gevra of ek sal likes om ouens te meet wat ringe deur die neus, gatte deur die ore en skiere in die gesig het. Ek het hom gesê: "As dit is, hulle maak nie dood nie en hul' jaag nie weg nie." So hy het my gevra of my bene is sterk om te kan vat aan sy linkerbo mou/sy. Hy het my gevra wat sien ek as die son opkom. Ek het hom gesê: "Ek sien niks nie." Hy het my gevra wat sien ek as die son sak. "Ek sien tot 'n groen boom met twee klippe." Toe ek by die boom kom sien ek dis nie net 'n boom nie, dis die ouens se rusplek. Ek het op die rooi klip gesit en afgegly en ek het op die spierwit klip gaan sit. Hy vat uit die hawersak 'n khaki cloth/flag met drie kleur — grasgroen, spierwit en bloedrooi (the green, red and white of the flag of 28). Hy het die kanna-kanna (knife that killed Rooiland) by bloedrooi gesit, die banana op

131

die spierwit gesit, en die snuff (African sangoma tradition of snuff taking) op die groen gesit. En hy het my gevra of my bene sterk is om te gaan vat op die kanna-kanna. En ek het hom gewys. En dan eet ek die piesang (lekker en soet) en dan ek het twee keer gesnuif en twee keer geneus. Hy het weer die khaki lap opgerol en weer in die khaki hawersak gesit. En hy het my gevra wat sien ek as die son opkom. Ek sê vir hom: "Ek sien niks nie." En hy het my gevra wat sien ek as die son sak. Ek het hom gesê: "Ek sien tot 'n donker grot." (The cave where the Silver Line are initiated sexually). Ons het daar geslaap vir 'n jaar.

📖

After this *die chaila moet hulle volmaak soos die geskryf is* – the new recruit cannot change his mind, he must fulfil his obligation as it is written. The gatekeeper will prevent any disruption of proceedings.

The Homecoming – the first page of the Book of 26

The litany of the Camp of 26 also gives the new recruit a choice. He can decide to opt for any of the three Camps. It includes direct references to the work of all three gangs and describes their flags, tents and other symbols. It can be studied in the vernacular in the addendum. The emphasis is on the *right* thumb and the *right* side to indicate that a 26 shuns sex with other men. As with the 28s they avoid mentioning names or even the numbers of the three Camps.

The Voice of Grey

I was a *frans* and I slept in the bush. I had everything that I wanted right up to some money of my own. Then two men came and robbed me with a clear conscience (no violence). They left me a bit for myself, but when that was used up I had to go and look for work. (He is going to look for the men who robbed him because, when they return, they will take everything he has and leave him nothing.) I found myself on the left-hand side of the road. In the distance I saw a grass-green tent and as I got closer a voice stopped me. I stood stock-still and I saw a grass-green flag with a thick red line and the Number (28). The voice enquired of me who I was and what I wanted. (Compare with Pawule's experience when he goes to find work in the mines.) So I replied that I was a youngster looking for work. The voice said: "The work here is bitter and hard and we work day and night with blood. We go to bed with the thought of poison (sex) and blood and rise up with the thought of poison and blood. (Clearly he meets the Bloodline of the 28s.) I told him I would go on looking for a job and that I'd come back if I did not find one.

Then I crossed the road and walked on the right-hand side. As I walked I saw in the far, far distance a blood-red tent. As I approached a voice stopped me. I stood stock-still and looked up. I saw a blood-red flag with seven six-pointed stars, two crossed-blades pointing upwards, a blood-red horn and the Number (27). The voice searched and asked who I was and what I was looking for. I replied that I was an innocent young man looking for a job. Then the voice answered: "The work here is hard, here we work day and night with blood, we sleep and stand up with blood on our minds and at any moment we will grab a red hot gun and go to the mountains. When we come back we have used up all our energy." I replied that I'd continue looking for work and would come back if I did not get a job. The voice suggested that, in the direction in which I was going, I would find my brothers. (Camp of 26 by implication.) So I kept on the right-hand side of the road and in the distance saw a pure-white tent. As I neared the tent a voice stopped me. I stood still and looked up and saw a pure-white flag with a thin red line and a coin and the Number (26). The voice searched and asked who I was and what I was looking for. I replied that I was a *frans* looking for a job. Then my brothers replied that the work was good and hard: "Here we work day and night with money. We sleep and stand up with money on our minds." I replied that I really fancied the work that they did. Then the brothers took me and stood me at the gates for six years. The sixth year the gates opened with *salute aan nommer*. Two men came to fetch me (Glas and Draad/Inspector and Captain One) and took me to a man who stood at attention with one stripe facing downwards on his right-hand sleeve. These two men lifted their right thumbs in a salute: "Nogidela, you address Inspector and Captain One. This youngster on the right-hand side is called to the Twelve Points. *Speel hom op met lyn van nommer.* Salute!" (see addendum for The Homecoming in the vernacular)

The last section of this 26 litany mirrors the experience of Pawule Mambazo when he arrives at the mine (prison) gates, whereas the litany of the 28 Gang indicates that the men are still living in Pawule's cave in the mountains. The reciting of The Homecoming of the Camp of 26 is followed immediately by reciting the details of the Initiation Ceremony (from p.89). In this way the new recruit identifies where he belongs, the oath that he takes, the tasks he is expected to perform and the details of the hierarchy of his Camp, the roles of the seniors and the uniforms that they wear. It may be assumed, but has not yet been confirmed, that the recruit for the Camp of 27 recites a similar Homecoming to that of the 26s.

blameless and blameworthy

The Number Gangs have been able to sustain their existence in South African prisons due to the nature of communal prison life and the overcrowded conditions in South African prisons, the richness of the gang mythology – which speaks directly to the collective unconscious – and the fact that the gangs are extremely well organised and apply tried and tested business principles.

South African prisons are overcrowded, usually by 50 to 100%. South Africa also has a very high incarceration rate — four out of every thousand men (mostly Black and Coloured) will go to jail compared with under two per thousand in first-world countries. The recently introduced minimum sentencing procedure means those who are incarcerated are going to prison for longer and longer periods — at any one time over 50 000 inmates will be serving sentences of over ten years. As a result ninety men will sleep in a cell designed for thirty individuals. There will be one toilet. They will be locked up in unsanitary conditions with no activities, other than television, for up to seventeen or eighteen hours per day. The noise level itself is quite unbearable. For most there is no escape from the mindless boredom unless they enter a mythical world of fantasy that provides them with weapons, uniforms, status, brotherhood and even the excitement of war.

If they join a gang they have a sense of entitlement when in competition for scarce commodities with non-gang members. They are feared by other prisoners. Loneliness, one of the most awful aspects of prison life, is banished.

The continued success of the gangs can also be ascribed to the fact that the gangs operate in every prison in the country. They have the same programmes running in each one of these prisons. They are waiting to greet new arrivals with open arms.

Correctional Services have no across the board rehabilitation policy, they have no *effective* across the board substance abuse programmes and no drug-free cells. They have no ability to protect inmates despite what the South African constitution states about keeping prisoners in safe and humane conditions.

big brother

Prisons are overflowing with anti-social and psychopathic individuals. The prison-gang system was designed by Nongoloza to accommodate the anti-social personality. The anti-social, like Nongoloza himself, have a life history that demonstrates most (or all) of the following: poor interpersonal relationships, poor work and school performance, criminal behaviour or conflict with authority (often from a very young age), mores not in keeping with the wider community, abuse of substances, use of aliases, unhealthy use of fantasy, lots of acting-out behaviour, defective judgement, impulsive behaviour, inability to learn from past mistakes, ability to manipulate others, low anxiety unless in a dangerous situation, inability to project into the future, repetition of the same self-defeating behaviour patterns, low self-esteem, self-destructive urges and polymorphous-perverse sexual behaviour — sex can be viewed as *just another commodity* .

Joining a gang simplifies life for the prisoner. He is given a set of rules that determine exactly how he should relate to others in the group. At the same time the rigid discipline of the gangs – and the constant monitoring of the behaviour of gang members by their brothers – means that behaviour in prison is constantly controlled by an outside source. This helps very anti-social people, who seem to have poorly developed consciences, to cope in crowded surroundings with as little conflict as possible.

big business

If one understands corporate business practices then The Number will hold few secrets. It operates in a similar manner to the corporate world. It's big business with lots at stake and the commodities for sale are drugs and sex. The only major difference being that, when you get stabbed in the back, real blood flows. So don't make any mistakes!

The senior officers in The Number have the same expectations of new recruits as CEOs in large organisations have of their employees. They supply them with training and equip them with the knowledge, jargon and skills to do their jobs properly. Gang protocol ensures they behave in a disciplined and acceptable manner towards each other. If they want to avoid a disciplinary hearing then it's a case of — loyalty, respect, obedience without questioning, following protocol and communicating through the accepted channels according to rank and hierarchy. Those who work well are rewarded accordingly. If members excel and prove their worth, bringing themselves to the attention of the senior members in The Number, they will be singled out for special training. They will rise quickly through the ranks to join the Chief Executive Officers, participating with the big boys when the Twelve Points hold a board-meeting.

Not only does The Number constantly source new members for the gangs, but The Number works continuously at building capacity in its members. Correctional Services could well take a leaf out of the Makhulu Book of Nongoloza!

135

References:

Gear, Sasha & Ngubeni, Kindiza: Daai Ding: Sex, Sexual Violence and Coercion in Men's Prisons (Centre for the Study of Violence and Reconciliation: 2002)

Haysom, N.: Towards an Understanding of Prison Gangs (Institute of Criminology: UCT/1981)

Morgan, Ruth & Wieringa, Saskia: Tommy Boys, Lesbian Men and Ancestral Wives - female same-sex practices in Africa (Jacana: 2005)

Parker Lewis, H: The Prison Speaks: Men's Voices/South African Jails (ihilihili press: 2003)

Schurink, W.J. Schurink, E; Lötter, M: Deviance and Crime/Number Gangs in South African Prisons – an organisational perspective - Association for Sociologists in Southern Africa (University of Natal: 1986)

Van Onselen, Charles: The Regiment of the Hills (published in Studies in the Social and Economic History of the Witwatersrand 1886-1914) – New Nineveh (Longman N.Y.: 1982)

Addendum:
SABELA DIE NOMMER (translated in part within the text): The following was smuggled out of prison in written form over a period of time. I have corrected some obvious spelling mistakes and added a little punctuation to aid understanding. Being of a naturally suspicious nature I got two copies to ensure that nothing had been invented. There were only minor discrepancies. In brackets are the alternative Xhosa/Zulu words which have, in some cases, been replaced by Afrikaans words. The member is free to choose which word he uses e.g. ouens (Afrikaans) or madodas (Xhosa). Either is accepted by The Number.

Die Huistoekom/Langpad of 26: (translation in Chapter 11)
Ek was 'n frans ek het geslaap in die bos. Ek het alles gehad tot 'n kroon. Twee ouens (madodas) het by my gekom en my geroof met 'n skoon gedagte. Hulle los my 'n stukkie, die stukkie het opgeraak. Toe besluit ek om werk te gaan soek. Ek het my bevind in die linkerkant van die pad. Ek het in die vêrte 'n grasgroen tent gesien en soos ek die tent benader het het 'n stem my gehault, toe staan ek vas en sien 'n grasgroen vlag met 'n dik rooi lyn en die nommer (28). Die stem het my gevra wie is ek en wat soek ek.
Ek het gesê ek is 'n frans ek soek werk.
Hy sê die werk is bitter en swaar en ons gaan dag en nag te werke met bloed. Ons slaap met die gedagte van gif en bloed (gazi) en staan op met die gedagte van gif en bloed.
Ek het hom gesê ek sal nog aan werk soek, maar as ek nie kry nie sal ek terugkom. Toe oorkruis ek die pad en loop in die regtekant. Soos ek loop sien ek uit die vêrte 'n bloedrooi tent en soos ek die tent nader het 'n stem my gehault, ek het vasgestaan en opgekyk. Ek sien 'n bloedrooi vlag met sewe sespunt stêrre, twee kapsale oorkruis wat sonop wys, 'n bloedrooi horing en die nommer gestam (27). Die stem soek en vra my wie is ek en wat soek ek. Ek het gesê ek is 'n frans en ek soek werk. Toe sê hy die werk is swaar, hier gaan ons dag en nag te werke met bloed, ons slaap en staan op met die gedagte van bloed en enige tyd vat ons 'n vuurwarme skietyster en sak ons berge as ons terugkom dan is dit yskoud.
Ek het gesê ek sal nog aan werk soek, as ek nie kry nie sal ek terugkom. Die stem het my gesê daar waar ek gaan is daar ook broers van my.
Ek het aangehou in die regtekant van die pad in die vêrte sien ek 'n spierwit tent. Toe ek die tent nader toe 'n stem het my gehault, ek het vasgestaan en opgekyk en 'n spierwit vlag gesien met 'n dun rooi lyn met 'n kroon en die nommer gestam (26). Die stem het gesoek en gevra wie is ek en wat soek ek. Ek het gesê ek is 'n frans ek soek werk. Hulle het gesê die werk is lekker en swaar, hier gaan ons dag en nag te werke met kroon. Ons gaan slaap en staan op met die gedagte van kroon. Ek het gesê ek sal daarvan hou om die werke to doen wat julle doen. Hulle het my gevat en geplant by die hekke vir 'n ses jarred. Die sesde jaar die hekke het oopgegaan met salute aan nommer.

137

First time around the recruit is also given the following as a protection, prior to his full initiation, so that he cannot be recruited by another gang (the clothing differs from that which he wears as a soldier once initiated):
Twee manskape (Glas en Draad) het my phezula gevat tot voor 'n manskap wat staan op attention met een streep op sy regte bo-mou wat af wys. Die manskappe lig hulle regteduime: "Salute, Nogidela! Jy chaisana meet met Inspector en Kaptein Een met die malighta aan die regtekant wat Die Twaalf Punt (Shumielnambini) dingela (want). Speel hom op met lyn van Nommer. Salute!"
Hy (Nogidela) het my phezula tot voor 'n manskap wat staan op attention met twee strepe op sy regte bo-mou wat op wys. Hy het sy regteduim gelig, "Salute, Sgt Twee! Fondela jy chaisana met Nogidela kangaka met die malighta aan die regtekant wat die Twaalf-Punte dingena. Pakamiesa phezulu. Kom speel hom met lyn van Nommer."
Hy het sy regteduim gelig en gewys: "Salute, Nogidela!"
My phezula gebring tot voor 'n manskap wat staan op attention met drie strepe op sy regte bo-mou wat op wys. Hy het my 'n sfogiso (*corruption of the Zulu word siboniso/warning*) gewys is hoe wat ek sal "down" in die voorkant. Daai manskap het my phezula en gebring tot voor sy Sgt. One. Hy het my uitgeissue. (*The first time the inmate is clothed as a novice and issued with the same equipment Pawule got from the mine bosses.*) Hulle het my gevat en my gegee 'n paar bruin boots sonder veters en sonder stam, 'n khaki overall sonder knope en sonder stam, 'n khaki helmet, khaki baadjie, sonder band, sonder stam stamp en sonder stam voorkant en agterkant, 'n pik en 'n graaf . Met dit sal ek dig en sif, alles wat ek kry wat sterkmaak ek sal eerste kom by die Ouens van Sonop. (*A repetition of Pawule's experience when he reaches the mine.*)

Once accepted for initiation the recruit replaces the previous lines with the following: (refer to Chapter 10 and the Initiation Ceremony)
Twee manskappe het my benader, gevat aan my regtekant en ingemaseer met hulle tot voor 'n manskap (Nogidela) met een streep op sy regte bomou wat af wys. Daai twee manskappe het hulle regteduime gelig en gewys: "Salute, Nogidela! Hier is die malighta wat Die Twaalfpunte (dingela) wil hê. Ek pakamiesa, vat en speel hom met lyn van Nommer."
Nogidela het sy regteduim gelig en gewys: "Salute!" Hy het my gephezula aan die regtekant tot voor 'n manskap wat staan op (attention) met twee strepe op sy regte bomou wat op wys. Nogidela het sy regteduim gelig en gewys: "Salute, Sergeant-Two! Hier is die malighta wat die Twaalf-punte dingela (requires/summons), ek pakamiesa, vat en speel hom met lyn van Nommer."
Sergeant-Two het sy regte duim gelig en gewys: "Salute!" Hy't my gevat en 'n (fotisa) gewys hoe ek sal (down) in Die Twaalf-punte. Hy het my weer gebring tot voor 'n manskap wat staan op attention met drie strepe op sy regte bomou wat op wys. Hy het sy regteduim gelig en gewys: "Salute Sergeant-One! Hier is die malighta wat die Twaalf-punte dingela. Vat en speel hom met lyn van Nommer."

Sergeant-One het sy regteduim gelig en gewys: "Salute!" Hy het my gephezula en gebring tot voor sy Inspector One - 'n plek waar die (British) soldiers' clothes gestoor word in die kamp van Ses-en-Twintig - en uitgeissue 'n paar bruin boots, khaki broek, khaki baadjie, khaki helmet sonder band en stam. Met sy klaar (vedala) het hy my gebring tot voor 'n manskap wat staan op attention met drie-strepe op sy regte bo-mou met 'n star (magunya). Hy het sy regteduim gelig en gewys: "Salute, Sergeant-Major! Hier is die malighta in die regtekant wat die Twaalf-Punte pakamies chaisana. Ek pakamiesa, vat en speel hom met lyn van Nommer."

Major het pakamiesa en my gebenzula en toegesluit (baitela) voor sy stokkies vir ses minute om 'n dissipline vol te maak op my. Op die sesde minute het 'n manskap gekom met vier gunyas, twee aan weeskant. Hy het sy regteduim gelig en gewys: "Salute, Sergeant-Major! Soos my drade gegrens (boundaries breached) het, het ek kom wysraak. Die malighta, wat die 'punte want (dingela) is baitela voor jou stokkies, ek pakamiesa hom chaisana."

Major het gewys: "Salute, Kaptein Two!"

Kaptein-Twee, met die vier gunyas, het my gevat (phenzula) en gebring tot op 'n spierwit oppervlak, daar het ek gesien (fotcha) ses manskap sit kop-aan-kop. En my gevisinteer (searched) vir enige skerp voorwerpe wat die Twaalf Punte kan vedala (seermaak) en daar het ek gefotcha down ses manskap. (*Just as Pawule searches those who visit his cave.*)

Hy het sy regteduim gelig en gewys: "Salute (Madakeni)!"

Een manskap het opgestaan en gewys "Salute, Captain Two!"

Captain Two het gewys "Salute (Madakeni)! Die malighta is so kangaka wat die Twaalf-Punte dingela."

"Pakamiesa, Captain Twee, staan terug bokant jou pos. Ek pakamiesa, Kaptein, vir die werk wat jy gedala het. Ek pakamiesa, staan terug op jou spierwit pos."

En daar het ek fotcha een manskap staan op met agt gunyas (Madakeni) vier aan weeskante van sy skouers.

Madakeni's Speech:

Daai manskap het my phezula en dingela weet ek waar ek staan.

En ek wys hom: "Nakanye."

"Hier jy staan op die volle grond van 26."

Hy het gewys *salute down* en my gevra fondela ek waar ek down.

"Nakanye."

"Hier *down jy* in die volle Shumielnambini van die Nommer Twees in die Kamp Ses-en-Twintig. Fondela, hier is 'n hek vir in en nie 'n hek vir uit nie. Ons nooi of jaag nie weg nie. Het jy gekom met jou eie twee bene, jou volle hart en volle verstand? Is jy nog altyd sterkbene om sonop te gaan?"

"Salute! Ja."

"Dan sal ons nou gcwalisela en gcina met 'n one-time shotgun om die eerste manskap in die regtekant, Die Inspector, die volle amandla te gee om sy werk te volmaak."

"Salute! Stand up, one-time shotgun! Salute Inspector!"
Inspector, die eerste manskap in Madakeni se regtekant, het my phezula (gevat) en sy glas instel vir enige vuil brandmerke van ander nasies van verre lande. Met sy vedala het hy sy regteduim gelig en gewys: "Salute, Madakeni!"
Madakeni het my gephezula aan die regtekant: "Salute down!"
"Hosh Mafotcha! Wat kan jy wys met die glas wat jy gestel het op die manskap?"
"My glas change spierwit en ek pakamiesa Ses-en-Twintig."
"Hosh Doctor (Nyanga)! Wat wys jy op die werk van die Mafotcha?"
"Ek, Nyanga, pakamiesa Ses-en-Twintig."
"Hosh Judge! Wat wys jy op die Glas se werk?"
"Ek, Judge, pakamiesa Ses-en-Twintig."
"Hosh Lawyer (Mehli)! Wat wys jy op die werk van die Mafotcha?"
"Ek, Mehli, pakamiesa Ses-en-Twintig."
"Hosh, Mcobozi (document and file keeper), wat wys jy op die werk van die Mafotcha?"
"Ek, Mcobozi, pakamiesa Ses-en-Twintig."
"Fondela, soos Die Nommer pakamiesa, ek ook pakamiesa Ses-en-Twintig. Soos nou toe sal ons stand-up en gcina met 'n two-time shotgun om die tweede manskap in die regtekant die volle krag te gee om te gcina met sy werk. Salute up! Two-time shotgun!" (Two-time shotgun completed the doctor examines the new member in a parody of a medical examination; he holds his arms out while the doctor inspects his palms and takes one arm and bends it back to touch the shoulder.)
Nyanga het my phezula en sy (mabobas) gestel om te kyk of ek fit is. Hy het my gevra of ek aan enige siekte, kwale of gebrek lei en ek wys hom: "Nakanye."
 Kan ek 'n salute (tola) hear, (fotcha) see en sabela? Ek het hom gewys: "Salute!"
"Soos nou vat ek die lewendige stam van Ses-en-Twintig en brand dit binne in jou bloed (bomvana). Ek vat en sny jou krag en verdeel dit op in die kamp van Ses-en-Twintig, nobangela jy is nie sterker as jou broer nie en jou broer is nie sterker as jy nie. Jy is gewys en gegee om 'n vierde oog te gcina (do/dala/gcwalisela); daar waar jou broer nie fotcha en tola nie jy sal fotcha en tola; en daar waar jy nie fotcha en tola nie hy sal dit gcina. As jy moeg raak vir die werke van die huis sal ek daai stam kom haal met bloed."
Met sy vedala het hy (doctor) gewys: "Salute, Madakeni!"
En Madakeni het my weer phezula in sy regtekant en gewys: "Salute, down!"
"Hosh, Nyanga, wat kan jy wys op die werk wat jy gedala het?" asked Madakeni.
"Ek, Nyanga, soos ek my mabobas gestel het het dit fit gechange daai nobangela ek pakamiesa Ses (Stupa)."
"Hosh, Mafotcha, wat wys jy op die werk van die Nyanga?"
"Ek, Mafotcha, pakamiesa Stupa."
"Hosh, Judge, wat wys jy op die werk van die Nyanga?"
"Ek, Judge, pakamiesa Stupa."
"Hosh Mehli! Wat wys jy op die werk van die Nyanga?"
"Ek, Mehli, pakamiesa Stupa."

"Hosh, Mcobozi, wat wys jy op die werke van die Nyanga?"

"Ek, Mcobozi, pakamiesa Stupa."

"Soos Die Nommer pakamiesa by julle dan ek ook pakamiesa Stupa."

(Only Madakeni at the Twelve-Points can give permission for the recruit to give the 26 salute, to work for the 26s, to speak the gang language. Madakeni gives him the six rules/laws that may not be broken.)

Madakeni het my gewys: "Fondela (manje) nou jy is 'n madoda en dee's van 'n frans jy het die gelos (gatela) in die bos (hlatini). Ek, Madakeni, gee jou die voorreg (lungela) om 'n regte duim te kan lug, om 'n kroon te kyk vir jou en banhle madodas en om die madodas se tale te kan sabela. Jy is gegee van ses-en-twintig wette, maar jy sabela net van ses. (1)Jy sal nie maak en doen wat jy wil nie; (2)jy sal nie agter jou broer se boots sabela nie; (3)jy sal nie jou broer nwata balisa (lie) nie; (4)'n frans waarsku jy twee keer en die derde keer sal Die Nommer jou wys hoe om te dala; (5)cops (mapoeza) se skoon werke sal jy respek en dissipline, behalwe sy vuil werke; (6)jy gaan vedala (die with your brothers if necessary) saam jou broer nomakanjani die nobangela, no matter what is demanded of you. (nobangela from banga meaning cause/demand). Jy is ook gegee van ses werke, waarvan jy vier sabela en twee is op slasluka, maar ek is nie die manskap wat jou skoolgee in jou werke nie. Daar is 'n manskap in die lyn van die nommer wat jou sal skool met jou werke. Toe sal ek jou nou fondela (know) as 'n full-force soldier in die kamp van Stupa. Ek sal jou fondela met 'n paar bruin boots binne en buite gestam ses-en-twintig, 'n paar spierwit puttees - dun rooi lyn met die stam stupa, ses buckles, drie aan weeskant. Khaki broek, khaki baadjie - ses spierwit knope, dun rooi lyn met die stam stupa. Bionet in die linkersy met 'n spierwit handvatsel - dun rooi lyn met die stam stupa. A point 303 geweer oor jou regteskouer met ses-en-twintig patrone - 25 in die magasyn, een in die loop. Twenty-six, volgens Nommer! Khaki helmet, spierwit band dun rooi lyn, kroon en nommer gestam ses-en-twintig. Spierwit specialboek - 26 spierwit blaaie, dun rooi lyn, kroon en nommer gestam 26. Swart pen en wit pen - swart vir die wrong en wit vir die right. En dit is so wat ek jou sal fondela in die kamp Ses-en-Twintig as 'n full-force soldier."

Madakeni presents the uniforms and roles of the officers: (refer to Chapter 10)

"Die **manskap** in die regtekant van my sal jy fondela as **Mafotcha 2** in die Kamp 26. Jy sal hom fondela met 'n paar private skoene binne en buite gestam 26, private broek, private baadjie, met 6 spierwit knope, dun rooi lyn met die nommer gestam 26, 'n spierwit boeksetsel met 'n dun rooi lyn en die stalala coboza Mafotcha 2, 'n spierwit borsspeldt op sy regte bo-kapel, dun rooi lyn met die stalala coboza Mafotcha 2, 'n private pet met 'n spierwit band, 'n dun rooi lyn met 'n kroon en die nommer gestam 26, spierwit boekspecial met 26 spierwit blaaie, dun rooi lyn kroon en nommer gestam 26, swart pen, en wit pen, swart vir die wrong en wit vir die salute. Die **tweede manskap** sal jy fondela as **Nyanga 2** in die Kamp 26. Jy sal hom fondela met 'n spierwit boekstelsel in sy regte hand, dun rooi lyn met die stalala coboza Nyanga 2, 'n spierwit borsspeldt op sy regte bo-kapel dun rooi lyn en die stalala coboza Nyanga 2. Die **derde manskap** sal jy fondela as **Judge 2** in die Kamp 26. Jy sal hom fondela met 'n spierwit boekstelsel in sy regte hand met 'n dun rooi lyn en die stalal coboza Judge 2. Jy sal hom ook fondela met 'n spierwit borsspeldt op sy regte bo-kapel, dun rooi lyn en die stalala coboza Judge 2. Die **vierde manskap** sal jy fondela as **Mehli 2**. Jy sal hom fondela met 'n spierwit boekstelsel in sy regte hand, dun rooi lyn met die stalala coboza Mehli 2 in die Kamp 26. Jy sal hom fondela met 'n spierwit borsspeldt op sy regte bo-kapel, dun rooi lyn met die stalala coboza Mehli 2. Die **vyfde manskap** sal jy fondela as **Mcobozi 2** in die Kamp 26. Jy sal hom fondela met 'n spierwit boekstelsel in sy regte hand met 'n dun rooi lyn en die stalala coboza Mcobozi 2. Jy sal hom ook fondela met 'n spierwit borsspeldt op sy regte bo-kapel dun rooi lyn en die stalala coboza Mcobozi 2. Vir my wat **Madakeni** is sal jy fondela met 'n paar bruin boots binne en buite gestam 26, spierwit gamaskes dun rooi lyn met die stam 26, ses buckles, drie-drie aan weeskante; gabedine broek, gabedine baadjie met ses spierwit knope, dun rooi lyn met die stam 26. Bionet in die linkersy met 'n spierwit handvatsel, dun rooi lyn met die stam 26. Bruin revolver holster in die regte sy, met 'n revolver, ses patrone, vyf in die magasyn en een in die loop. Ses volgens Nommer! Bloedrooi band op my regte bo-mou gestam **Fighting in die Kamp 26**, agt magunyas vier-vier aan weeskante van my skouers, gabedine pet met 'n spierwit band, dun rooi lyn, kroon en nommer gestam 26, spierwit special boek, dun rooi lyn met kroon en nommer gestam 26. Swart en wit pen, swart vir wrong en wit vir die right (salute). Vir **jou sal ek fondela** (repetition - not sure if deliberate or a mistake; the special book is omitted) as 'n full force **soldaat** met 'n paar bruin boots binne en buite gestam 26, spierwit puttees met 'n dun rooi lyn en die nommer gestam 26, ses buckles drie-drie weeskante; khaki broek en khaki baadjie met ses spierwit knope, dun rooi lyn en die nommer gestam 26, bionet in die linkersy, spierwit handvatsel, dun rooi lyn en die stam 26; point 303 haal geweer oor die regteskouer, 26 patrone, 25 in die magasyn een in die loop. Two-six volgens Nommer! Khaki helmet, spierwit band met 'n dun rooi lyn, kroon en nommer gestam 26. Swart en wit pen, swart vir wrong en wit vir die right. Gcwala wat die Twaalf-punte sy werk gedala het sal ek een en elk nikeza wat hulle kan wysmaak."

Madakeni now asks each of his officers in turn whether they agree with what they have just witnessed:
"Hosh Mafotcha, wat kan jy wys op die werk van Die Twaalf-Punte?"
"Ek, Mafotcha, pakamiesa met die werk van Die Twaalf-Punte!"
"Hosh, Nyanga, wat kan jy wys op die werk van Die Twaalf-Punte?"
"Ek, Nyanga, pakamiesa met die werk van Die Twaalf-Punte!"
"Hosh, Mehli, wat kan jy wys op die werke van Die Twaalf-Punte?"
"Ek, Mehli, pakamiesa met die werke van Die Twaalf-Punte!"
"Hosh, Judge, wat kan jy wys op die werke van Die Twaalf-Punte?"
"Ek, Judge, pakamiesa met die werke van Die Twaalf-Punte."
"Hosh, Mcobozi, wat kan jy wys op die werke van Die Twaalf-Punte?"

"Ek, Mcobozi, pakamiesa met die werke van die Twaalf-Punte en is op daai nobangela vat ek die manskap se stalala as 'n full-force soldaat en coboza die in die boeke van my met 'n general salute en salute."

"Ek, wat Madakeni is, pakamiesa ook met die werke van die Twaalf-Punte. Wat die werke met salute gepikelela het dan sal ek die manskap opspeel met lyn van Nommer tot op sy spierwit pos. Hosh, Kaptein! Gcwala die Twaalf-Punte het met salute sy werk gedala en die manskap sal jy fondela as 'n full-force soldaat in die Kamp van 26 en ek pakamiesa jy moet hom op speel met lyn van Nommer tot op sy spierwit pos."

Then those in the lower ranks introduce their uniforms and roles:
Kaptein het my gebenzula en my nikeza met wie chaisana ek: "Vir my sal jy fondela as **Kaptein-Twee** in die Kamp van 26. Jy sal my ken met 'n paar bruin boots binne en buite gestam 26, spierwit gamaskes, dun rooi lyn met die stam 26. Ses buckles, drie aan weeskante. Gabadine broek, gabadine baadjie, ses spierwit knope met 'n dun rooi lyn en die nommer gestam 26. Biyonet in die linkersy met 'n spierwit handvatsel en 'n dun rooi lyn en die nommer gestam 26. Bruin revolver-holster in die regtesy skangaka met 'n revolver, ses patrone, vyf in die magasyn, een in die loop. Ses volgens Nommer! Spierwit draadloos in my regtehand met die stalal gecoboza Kaptein-Twee in die Kamp 26. Spierwit cane onder my regteblad met 'n dun rooi lyn en die nommer gestam 26. Vier gunyas, twee aan weeskante van my skouers. Gabadine pet met 'n spierwit band, dun rooi lyn en kroon en stam 26. Spierwit special boek met 'n dun rooi lyn, kroon en stam 26. Swart pen en wit pen, swart vir wrong en wit vir salute (right). Vir jou sal ek fondela met 'n paar bruin boots binne en buite gestam 26; spierwit puttees met 'n dun rooi lyn en die stam 26; khaki broek, khaki baadjie met ses spierwit knope, dun rooi lyn en die stam 26; biyonet in die linker sy met 'n spierwit handvatsel, dun rooi lyn en die stam 26; point 303 haal geweer oor die regteskouer met 26 patrone, 25 in die magsyn, een in die loop. Two-six volgens Nommer! Khaki helmet, spierwit band met 'n dun rooi lyn en kroon en stam 26; spierwit specialboek, 26 spierwit blaaie, dun rooi lyn, kroon en stam 26; swart en wit pen, swart vir wrong en wit vir right." Met Kaptein se vedal het hy my phezula en opgespeel. Hy het gewys: "Hosh Sergeant Major! Gwala die werk van die Twaalf-Punte het pikelela (went) met salute en vedala (finished) met salute en die manskap in die regtekant sal jy fondela (recognise) as 'n full-force soldaat. Ek pakamiesa jy moet hom phezula en opspeel tot op sy spierwit pos."

Sergeant Major het gepakamiesa en my nikeza: "Fondela jy met wie chaisana jy?" En ek het gewys: "Nakanye."

"Vir my sal jy fondela as **Sergeant Major** en is ek wat die dissipline gcwalisela in die Kamp van 26. Jy sal my fondela met 'n paar bruin boots binne en buite gestam 26; spierwit gamaskes met 'n dun rooilyn en die stam 26; ses buckles, drie-drie aan weeskante; gabedine broek en baadjie, ses spierwit knope, dun rooi lyn met die nommer gestam 26; bayonet in die linkersy met 'n spierwit handvatsel, dun rooi lyn en die nommer gestam 26; bruin rewolwer holster in die regtesy met 'n

143

rewolwer; ses patrone, vyf in die magasyn een in die loop. Ses volgens Nommer! Drie strepe op my regte bo-mou met 'n magunya; gabadine pet, spierwit band, dun rooit lyn kroon en nommer gestamp 26; spierwit special book, 26 spierwit blaaie dun rooi lyn kroon en nommer gestam 26; swart en wit pen, swart vir wrong en wit vir right. Vir jou sal ek fondela as 'n full-force soldaat in die kamp (26)." Hy't my gephezula tot voor 'n manskap. Met sy kangaka kom het hy sy regteduim gelig en sabela: "Salute, **Sergeant-Een**. Die Twaalfpunte het vedala met salute, die manskap in die regtekant sal jy fondela as 'n full-force soldaat, pakamiesa phezula hom en speel hom op met lyn van Nommer tot op sy spierwit pos."

Hy't sy regteduim gelig: "Salute!" Hy't my phezula: "Fondela jy met wie jy chaisana?"

"Nakanye."

"Jy chaisana met **Sergeant-Een** en vir my sal jy fondela met 'n paar bruin boots, binne en buite gestamp 26; spierwit puttees, dun rooi lyn, nommer stam 26, ses buckles drie-drie weeskante; khaki broek; khaki baadjie, ses spierwit knope dun rooi lyn, nommer gestam 26; bayonet in die linker sy, spierwit handvatsel, dun rooi lyn nommer gestam 26; bruin rewolwer holster in die regtesy met 'n rewolwer, ses patrone, vyf in die magasyn een in die loop. Ses volgens Nommer! Drie strepe op my regte bo-mou wat op wys; khaki helmet, spierwit band, dun rooi lyn kroon en nommer stam 26; swart pen, wit pen, wit vir right en swart vir wrong. (Pens imply presence of the *special* book (the brain), although it is not always mentioned.) Vir jou sal ek fondela as 'n full-force soldaat in die Kamp van 26." Met sy vedala het hy my phezula tot voor 'n manskap. Hy't sy regte duim gelig: "Salute Sergeant-Twee! Fondela die Twaalf-Punte het vedala general, met general salut en salute. Die manskap in die regtekant sal jy fondela as 'n full-force soldaat in Die Kamp. Pakamiesa, phezula hom en speel hom tot op sy spierwit pos."

Sergeant-Twee het my phezula: "Fondela jy met wie jy chais?"

"Nakanye."

"Jy chais met **Sergeant-Twee**. Ek is die manskap wat jou elke sesde jaar sal vat top op die drilling baan. Vir my sal jy fondela met 'n paar bruin boots binne en buite gestam 26; spierwit puttees, dun rooi lyn, nommer gestam 26, ses buckles, drie-drie weeskante; khaki broek en baadjie, ses spierwit knope, dun rooi lyn nommer stam 26; bayonet in die linksy, spierwit handvatsel, dun rooi lyn, nommer stam 26; bruin rewolwer holster in die regtesy met 'n rewolwer, ses patrone, vyf in die magasyn, een in die loop. Ses volgens Nommer! Twee strepe op my regte bo-mou wat op wys; khaki helmet, spierwit band, dun rooi lyn, kroon en nommer stam 26; spierwit boekspecial; spierwit boekblaaie dun rooi lyn, kroon en nommer stam 26; swart en wit penne, swart vir wrong, wit vir right. Vir jou sal ek fondela as 'n full-force soldaat in Die Kamp." Hy't my phezula tot voor n manskap en sy regteduim gelig: "Salute 'gidela! Die Twaalf-Punte het vedala met 'n general salute en salute. Die manskap in die regtekant sal jy fondela as 'n full-force soldaat in die Kamp 26. Pakamiesa hom phezula en speel hom op met lyn van Nommer. Salute!"

Nogidela het my phezula: "Salute, down! Fondela hier waar jy down, down jy in die volle skole van N'gidela. Vir my sal jy fondela as jou 'gidela. Vir my sal jy fondela met 'n paar bruin boots binne en buite gestam; spierwit puttees, dun rooi lyn, nommer stam 26, ses buckles drie-drie weeskant; khaki broek, khaki baadjie, ses spierwit knope, dun rooi lyn nommer stam 26; bayonet in die linkersy, spierwit handvatsel dun rooi lyn, nommer stam 26; bruin rewolwerholster in die regte sy, met n rewolwer, ses patrone, vyf in die magasyn, een in die loop. Ses volgens Nommer! Keys vyf-en-twintig aan 'n bos in my regtesy. Een in my regtehand gestamp masterkey (keys: 19 are for the leaders and six for the soldiers and one masterkey); een streep op my regte bo-mou wat af wys; khaki helmet, spierwit band dun rooi lyn, kroon en nommer gestam 26; spierwit boekspecial, 26 spierwit boekblaaie, dun rooi lyn, kroon en nommer gestam 26; swart en wit penne, swart vir wrong en wit vir right. Vir jou sal ek fondela met 'n paar bruin boots binne en buite gestam 26; spierwit puttees, dun rooi lyn, nommer stam 26; khaki broek; khaki baadjie, ses spierwit knope, dun rooi lyn, nommer stam 26; bayonet in die linkersy, spierwit handvatsel, dun rooi lyn, nommer stam 26. Point 303 haal geweer oor jou regteskouer, 26 patrone, 25 in die magasyn een in die loop. 26 volgens Nommer! Khaki helmet met 'n spierwit band, dun rooi lyn, kroon en nommer gestam 26; spierwit boekspecial, 26 spierwit boekblaaie, dun rooi lyn, kroon en nommer gestam 26; swart en wit pen, swart vir wrong en wit vir right. Fondela, jy word geskool met 26 wette waarvan jy van 6 sabela. Jy sal nie maak en doen nie, jy sal nie agter jou tweede broer se boots sabela nie, jy sal nie jou tweede broer nwata bhalesa nie, 'n frans sal jy twee keer waarsku, die derde keer sal die Nommer jou wys hoe dala jy. Mapoeza se skone werke sal jy dissipline behalwe sy vuil werke. Jy vedala met jou broer onder daai spierwit vlag, dun rooi lyn, kroon en nommer gestam 26, nomakanjane hoe die nobangela lyk. Ek skool jou met ses werke waarvan jy van vier sal sabela, twee is op slasluka. Jy is dag en nag op 'n pos, kyk uit vir enige gevaar wat die kamp kan benader, jy kyk 'n kroon met jou Twee-Ses vir jou en die (umkhosi), van 26 jy werk jou op met 'n kroon en nommer tot op die pos van 'n 'gidela, twee op slasluk Glas vir Glas, Draad vir Draad. Ek het 'n tele van ses nommers op my blackboard. Salute! Tele van manskap, tele van kroon, tele van gebruike, een en elke nommer onderkant die een streep. Salute! Fondela soos nou sal ek jou phezula en plant tussen my en Sgt. Twee op nobangela ek skool jou met een en elke nommer onderkant die een streep en Sgt. Twee gcwalisela elke sesde jaare die drilling. Salute! Stand-at-ease! Attention! Stand-at-ease! Attention! Salute!"

Phambuka Songaqo: (The Crossroads: translated and discussed in Chapter 11)
Jare terug (1812) skangaka in 'n kraal in Mampondweni was 'n wyse man met die stalala (names) Paul Mambazo en sy nozala (parents). Sy nonzala was al by die vedala en was nie meer skangaka om te jigijela vir hulle wat sterk maak nie. Daai nobangela het hy gekyk om daai sterk maak te jikijela. Gcwala soos hy by die jikjela gewees het vir sterk maak het hy hom wys raak mapoeza van die myne kom skangaka om mense te phezula vir die slasluka van die myne. Gcwala soos die

mense weer gelandela het was hulle nie almal skangaka nie en die mfazis van die madodas het gekala nyembezi. Gcwala met daai hele slasluka het hulle gefotsisana (discussed) en daai wyse man was uitgehaal om te jikijela (to go right into and see and make a full enquiry) watter slasluka daleka met die mense wat nie weer landela nie. Paul Mambazo het gepikelela by die myne en by die hekke van myne het hy gechaisana met twee mapoezas wat skangaka gewees het met 'n binoculars en 'n draadloos.

Hulle het hom genikeza waarna toe hy op pad is, wie is hy, en wat soek hy.

"Ek is Paul Mambazo, ek soek na werk."

Die mapoeza met die draadloos het gekoppel tot in die myne en die nommer gespeel. Hy was gesit by die hekke vir sewe jare om te kyk of hy fit is vir die werke van die myne. Met die vedala van die sewe jarre het mapoeza hom gevat tot binne in die myne en daar was gekyk of hy die hitte kan staan van die myne, om hom in 'n grot te sit waar die hitte gestel kan raak.

Hy is fit vir die werke en was gegatela 'n paar bruin boots, khaki overall, khaki helmet gekoppel met 'n lig, 'n pik en 'n graaf en 'n sif en: "Met die sal jy dig en sif. Die wat salute het sal jy skangaka bring."

Hy was gepikelela tot onder in die myne wat ons memeza die (deep level). Soos hy te werke gegaan het in die deep level was daar ook mense wat skangaka gewees wat ook nie mekaar verstaan deur die verskillende tale wat hulle gepraat het. Maar raak wys, die Paul Mambazo het hy 'n manskap gechaisana wat al lankal skangaka in die myne is, wat almal fondela as Madala-One (The First One). Soos hulle gefotsisana het by die number wat hom skangaka bring, was daar ook 'n nommer gedala om almal daai tale te vat en een te maak wat ons sal memeza (fanikalo). Die jarre en minute toe almal mekaar chaisana was daar gefotsisana op die mense wat so vedala gaan en daar is niks wat mapoeza dala om daai mense te versterk nie. Hy het ook gechaisana met (witbene) van die mense wat nie weer gelandela het in die Mpondo nie. Hy en Madala-One het gefotsisana en almal daai ander nasies gechaisana om 'n slasluka te kan dala in die myne en op mapoeza en te getela by die myne met een en elk wat sterk maak. Daar was jarred gesny en hy het hom eers opgewerk tot by die boeke en kantore van mapoeza. Soos hy by die kantore (mafias/office) gewerk het, het hy die slasluka gebalesa met lyn tot binne in die deep level om te die jarred sal did nommer daleka en een en elk was gephezula wat sterk maak soos kroon (money), 'n boek met almal se stalazas wat so witbene gepikelela het, hulle het ook gepikelela met goud. Pawule het drade gebreek. Mapoeza het hulle vedala, en mapoeza se honde, terwyl hulle drade bebreek het.

Die Pawule het weer gepikelela tot in Mpondweni by sy kraal en sy nozala was nie meer skangaka nie, hy het gepikelela by nog 'n wyse man in sy kraal, met stalala (siazi) en is hy wat hom gewys het dat sy nozala witbene is en hy het die Pawule sy nozala gewys om te dala met 'n "one-time shotgun en a two-time shotgun" en hom wys gemaak met 'n spiel (mirror). Met hulle vedala het siazi hom wysgemaak om te gatela uit Pondoland uit vir jarred op nobangela die wat hy gedala het by die myne sal mapoeza hom vedala as hulle hom sal chais. Hy het toe almal met salute gegatela in Pondoland en die berge ingevlug. Soos hy gepikelela het het hy kom chais met in skeer in die berg. Hy het in die skeer gepikelela en kom kry met 'n grot wat hy in die dissipline gesit het en daar was hy skangaka vir jarred. Met sy vedala om die grot in dissipline te sit het hy alles wat sterk maak gebaitela en op 'n spierwit klip gaan sit voor die grot en die's ingegaan van 'n gebruike nommer.

Hy was ook skangaka met 'n binoculars wat hy die vier hoeke van die wêreld meen gejikijela het en so het hy ook 'n plaas gefondela waar 'n mapoeza met die stalala Rabie skangaka is met sy (queen) wife. Daar was ook 'n bees en nog 'n klomp ander beeste. Fondela daar was een bul skangaka wat die mense vedala het wat die wette van die Rabie oortree het.

Soos hy weer skangaka gewees het op daai spierwit klip en die vier hoeke van die wêreld gejikijela het en ook 'n gebruike gevoliesh het, het daar 'n stofwolk uit die vêrte verskyn en hy het die stofwolk gehault en gevra: "Wie is jy waar qamka jy en waar pikelela jy."

Die stem het gewys: "My stalala is Skalaka ek kom van Springs en ek is op pad myne toe om te spanga (work)."

Die Pawule Mambazo het hom gewys: "Ek is Paul Mambazo ek qamka van Pondoland en raak wys ek qamka van die myne en een en elk wat sterk maak was gebenzula en daar was drade gebreek. Ek sal pakamiesa jy moet skangaka in my regtekant. As jy sterkbene is om met my te koppel kan jy een en elk met die wat ek meen staan saam ingaan."

Hy het hom een en elk gefotsisa wat salute het en hy het gekoppel met die Pawule Mambazo.

Hy, die Pawule, het hom gevisinteer (visit) en gebenzula (removed) 'n kapsaal en gepikelela tot binne die grot. Hy het hom umhlaba (ground/earth) gegatela en hulle het gisitha (they sat) en gevoliesh (ate). Met die eerste strale het hulle gewuka (vuka/awake) en die dissipline vol gaan maak by die rivier wat ons memenja (memeza) die Mooi Rivier. Met hulle vedala het hulle weer skangaka gepikelela by die grot. Die jarred het gepikelela en toe die Pawule was skangaka op daai spierwit klip toe qamka daar nog 'n stofwolk uit die vêrte sien. Hy het die stofwolk gehault en hom gevra wie hy is, waar qamka hy, en waarna toe hy op pad is.

"Ek is Nongoloza, ek qamka van Dalakubay en ek pikelela by die myne."

Die Pawule het hom gewys: "Ek is die Paul Mambazo, ek qamka van Pondoland en ek qamka van die myne en een en elk wat salute het het hy gebenzula, want mapoeza se werke het nie salute nie. Ek sal pakamiesa jy moet skangaka is in my regtekant en koppel met die wat ek meen bymekaar is."

Hy het hom een en elk gefotisa wat salute het en hy het gekoppel met die Pawule Mambazo. Die Pawule het hom gewys met die wat hy vir die jarre bymekaar is en wat gedaleka het by die myne.

Soos die jarred gepikilela het het die Pawule gekyk om hulle te steur by die plaas met die stalala (Leiland), om te jigijela of hulle rêrig sterkbene met hom is. Die sewende jarred het hy hulle gewys om te pikelela by daai plaas en daai bul te vedala en skangaka te bring die bul se horings en bovana en die gal van mapoeza.

"Daai bul sal julle fondela met 'n ring deur sy neusgat, gate deur die ore en skeure deur die gevreet (face/head/muzzle) en hy is alleen skangaka in 'n kraal."

Hy het hulle kapsale gegatela en hulle het gepikelela. Met die qamka van hulle by die plaas het hulle daai mapoeza vedala en die gal gephenzula. Hulle het toe die bul ook vedala, die bovana (gazi) gebenzula, die horings en Nongoloza het sy eie goed gedala en die vel gephenzula (gebenzula). Ngkilikityane het hom gewys om nie die vel to phenzula nie, want Pawule het nie gesabela van die vel nie. Hy het vir Ngilikityane gewys dat die vel hom sal versterk vir nou en die jarred wat kom. Met hulle vedala het hulle weer gepikelela by die Pawule. Die Pawule het gepakamiesa met die wat hulle gedala het en hy het Nongoloza gevra hoe lyk die nobangela hy het die vel gephenzula het en hy het hom gewys dat dit hom sal versterk vir die jarred wat kom.

Die Pawule het die horing, gal, en die bovana (bloed) gevat en gemeng in die horing. Ngilikityane het die horing gevat en gedrink. Hy het dit uitgespoeg en die Pawule gewys dat die bloed salute het, maar die gal het nie salute nie. Nongoloza het gedrink en alles ingesluk en sabela: "GONQO!"

Dieselfde minute het die Paul (Pawule) gefotsa wie sal die een wees wat sal maak en doen en sy eie goed doen. Hy het hulle polse toe gesny en hulle gazilams (blood brothers) gemaak van mekaar. Hy het hulle ook gewys dat: "Julle nie weer polse sal sny nie, want die mense sal baleka (weghardloop). Soos die jarre pikelela sal julle manskappe chaisana wat sterkbene is om te pikelela met die wat julle meen bymekaar is en dis hulle polse wat julle nie sal sny nie, maar julle sal gcina (doen) met 'n one-time en two-time om hulle oë oop te maak. (1824) se jarred het hulle gazilams geraak en al twee het die sweer van agt (mzukwana-spohlongo) gelig. Die jarred het nog gepikelela en die Pawule het oud geraak en begin vedala (klaarraak/doodgaan). Een en elk wat die Pawule gesien (gefotsa) het vir die jarre wat hy van sy kraal af (gemarch) geloop het tot in die myne en tot by die jarre wat hy hulle gechaisana het even hy het tot binne die toekoms gefotsa met die wysheid wat hy gechaisana het. Hy het daai manskappe met een en elke nommer geskool wat hy duidelik gehad het by sy (special) gedagte op reason (nobangela) hy was by die dood (witbene). Hy het hulle ook gewys om te as hy nie hier (skangaka) is as hulle van die werk af kom raak wys julle sal my chaisana agter die berge van (Kahlumbe) Pietermaritzburg. Die jarred het gepikelela en hulle het weer gaan (myne) werk. Hulle het gephenzula die wat sterkmaak met violence (masalon/masalong). Die slasluka van roof en plinder was die werke wat hulle gedala het. Soos hulle weer teruggekom het van hulle werke af was daar goed gephenzula van die grot af waar hulle teruggegaan het. Hulle het gefotsisana waar hulle gestaan het dat Nongoloza sal werk in die nag en Ngilikityane sal werk in die dag: "So as ek werk deur die dag sal jy 'n pos vang op die slasluka wat skangaka is (the work - i.e. plunder - that is here), en as jy werk in die nag sal ek 'n pos vang op die wat skangaka is." Hulle het weer gepikelela met hulle werke en soos Nongoloza gaan werk het het hy malinas en malightas gekry wat sterkbene is met hom en ook in 'n lyn is wat koppel sterkmaak kyk. En soos Ngilikityane gaan

148

myne het, het hy ook gechais met (malightas) en (malinas) clever franse wat sterkbene is met hom. (note: Kilikijan is interchangeable with Ngilikityane) Hulle het gekoppel met hom soos die jarred gegaan het, maar soos Kilikijan van die werk (myne) afgekom het was Nongoloza skangaka met 'n frans met die name Magubaan. Nongoloza her Ngilikityane gebaleza waar kom (qamka) die frans. Hulle het 'n food (volish-three) geëet (gebetesa). Met hulle vedala om te eet het hulle mekaar gegroet en Nongoloza het gaan werk, en toe hy terugkom met die qamka van die strale was Ngilikityane al op 'n pos om hom te chaisana op die kruispad waar hulle mekaar groet en Nongoloza het hom gewys wat hy gewerk het en weer mekaar gepart (gegatela) het. Ngilikityane het gepikelela met sy werke en hy het in daai jaar (the same day) gekry dat die Pawule witbene is agter die berge van Kahlumbe en toe hy terugkom van die werke af, om die Nongoloza te wys, het hy kom kry dat die frans Magubaan onder Nongoloza se kombers (shebanga) is. Ngilikityane het Magubaan gevra hoekom hy nie ook gaan werk het nie en hy wys vir Ngilikityane dat Nongoloza hom gewys het dat hy nie twee werke kan doen nie. Hy vra hom hoe lyk die tweede werk en Magubaan wys: "Drie keer teen die klip kap dan spuit die water, en jy kan vir Nongoloza gaan vra ook." Nongoloza was bymekaar met 'n dissipline nommer. Toe hy fotsa Ngilikityane roep (beukel) hom tot op die kruispad het hy hom (geBritish) aangetrek (he armed himself) en geqamka. Ngilikityane het hom eers gegroet met die geloof van die sweer van spohlongo. Hy het hom gewys dat die Pawule witbene is en hom gevra van Magubaan. Nongoloza het hom gewys dat die frans sal hom versterk soos die jarre kom en dat hulle so lyk wat daai frans wys. Hy het hom gewys dat die Paul hulle ook nie geskool het met die wat hy gedala het. Ngilikityane het gebenzula by sy linkersy en Nogoloza geskiet (note: skiet does not imply shoot or the use of a gun but an injury or stab wound) en Nongoloza het hom gevra as hy hom wil vedala dan wie sal dan pikelela met die werke en Ngilikityane wys hom dat hy hom nie vedala nie, maar net die wrongs (nwatas). Nongoloza het gebaleka oor 'n grasgroen veld en die gazi (bloed) het geloop en 'n dik rooi lyn agter gelos en daar kom sy vlag lewendig. Die hemel en aarde het geskeer en daar het 'n stêr uit die lig geval tot voor op Magubaan se kop. Hy het Magubaan ook geskiet en so sal hy hom fondela met die bewysstuk van die skietmerk. Ngilikityane het hom gewys toe hy weer hom chais dat hulle moet die Pawule se witbene gaan begrawe en dink en leer (beka en funda) op die witbene. Hulle het eers Nongoloza met salute gedala met die (Nyanga) hospital items they had en gepikelela agter die berge om die Paul se bene te begrawe, beka en funda. Die berge was genoem Kahlumbe want dit was 'n stil plek waar ons met salute sal funda as 'n nommer nie duidelik kom nie en hier sal ons 'n duidelikheid kry. Ngilikityane was skangaka met 'n boombas geskryf (gebala). Hy het daai boombas gephezula en in die graf begrawe. Met hulle vedala het Nongoloza gepikelela weer Dalakubaai toe en Ngilikityane Springs toe, maar voor hulle mekaar los wys Ngilikityane hom dat hy moet fondela dat hy nie weer sal pikelela met die sweer van spohlongo nie, maar hy sal een finger (miniwe) weghaal: "En jy sal my fondela met die kenteken van seven (sixhenxe)."

149

A short lexicon of words/phrases in regular use in The Number:

(also included are the more obscure titles given to gang members – otherwise the titles/roles are discussed in the relevant chapters)

A

Aanhitser – reference to Magubaan as the kindler of desire

abathelisa – impersonation of officials

agter die berge – solitary confinement

amadodas – gang members with authority/men in the gang (as opposed to franse)

Amalitas – a name the gang used in the early days before the split (another version of People of the Stone from the word ilitye or stone)

Amapint – a pint milk bottle; the Lieutenant in the 28s and member of Gold Line/Division One/also known as The Germiston and Jim Crow

amasoja/amasoshi/masjallou – soldier/particularly the fighting line of the 28s/the Number 3s in the Gold Line of the 28s/the Bloodline

Arrow of Life – see Ngilikityane

B

babba – the father, the dominant sexual partner in the 28s

baitela/batela (voor jou stokkies) – to lock up

balisa nommer – authorised instructions

banana (from khanana/intense sexual desires) – see page 127 onwards and the initiation ceremony into the Silver Line in the Camp of 28

Band, Die – an alternative title for Madakeni/Madagunee, the 26 Fighting General

bandiet – prisoner

beka en funda – think and learn

benefit, a – a person who can offer or bring something that will strengthen the postion of the Camp/either food or money or drugs or intellect

berg toe (sak ons berge toe) – a reference to solitary confinement when the gang then rallies to support the member/it's a victory for the gang if someone is sent to a single cell in solitary having carried out a gang duty/the status of the gang member in solitary goes right up

betesa – food/eat (also: a diet/meal)

beukel – a call to the Crossroads to discuss issues of importance

Beukel, die – is keeper of the bugle (see die Draad)

Big Head, Jim – a reference to Jim Tanana the Giant with the Crooked Eyes who was Nongoloza's right hand man/possibly he was the man known as Ngilikityane and Ntlokonkulu, the latter title means the Big Head or Chief

Binoculars, the – see Inspector/die Glas/Mafotcha – this is an important gang position; the Binoculars/Inspector who, together with die Draad, must bear witness and accompany any member who carries out a duty that requires a man to stab

bitter en swaar – bitter and hard/a reference to work in the Camp of 28

black – this colour refers to death, using the black stamp means that the gang have sentenced someone to death; 26s refer to black when something is not done properly or when the rules have been broken

Blackboard, the – the gang member who keeps tally of what they have accumulated and also the teacher of the new recruits; on a Saturday he spins the board to reveal how the Camp has benefited over the last week; he does this in front of the members to prove his transparency – what is accumulated will also be shared with gang members who are to be transferred to another prison

Blacksmith – the Governor General in the Gold Line, Division One of the 28s/see Mtshali and also the Stairs

Bloodline – synonymous with Gold Line of the 28s/also Red Line

blood rank – the rank is vasgebrand in die bomvana, branded in through stabbing another person (either prisoner or warder) after being dutied

bloed/blood as in – bloedrooi/ manne van bloed – the 27 gang member
                          manskap van vleis en bloed – the 27 gang member
                          manskap van bloed – the 28 Gold Line
                          skoffel die grond met bloed – plough the ground with blood
                                    re-open the Gold Line of the 28s

Boek, Die/Book/Makhulu Book – the oral history of the gangs containing laws,
                          structure, rituals, anything to do with The Number

boekstelsel – oral memory relating to gang issues

boek special – the brain/memory/his head/sy kop

bomvana/bo'vana – veins/blood/life (see vasgebrand in die bomvana)

bomvana slasluka – when a brother is stabbed

bos, hy's in die – outside the gangs' camps, uninitiated into a Number Gang

brand, jy is gebrand/burned/gestamp – if you do not fulfil a duty/a docket is opened and unresolved issues must be cleared up/you are a marked man

brandmerke – tattoos (vuil brandmerke refers to tattoos from non-Number gangs)

British/geBritish – armed gang member/ready for war/can't turn back

broers/ons is broerse – brothers/we are part of the brotherhood

C

Camp, Die (Kamp) – the members talk of the Camps of 26/27/28 and prefer this word to gangs/but the word is synonymous with gang

Centre Post – a particular piece of turf honoured as territory; the Centre Post of 28 is the kitchen area and the Centre Post of the 27s is the exercise yard

cents – always translates as rands - 50c means R50

chais/chaisana/chaila – talk/consult/discuss with/address

chappies – tattoos

cave, the – a reference point in the Gang of 28 where sex takes place

Chosen One, the – a person who is sharp and ready (gesluip) for the work of 26

clerk/scribe – a gang position; see mabalang/rwenza/mcobozi

Colonel's child – can be used as an alternative to the title of Goliath 2

Crossroads, Die (Kruispad/ Phambuka Songaqo) – a metaphorical and historical meeting place when/where the gangs get together to discuss important issues based on the history of the gang; this is the place where Nongoloza and Ngilikityane confronted each other before they split up into the Camp of 28 and the Camp of 27

D

dala (see gedala/vedala) – do/perform

deep level/diep einde – steeped in the gang mythology/meaning he went right down into the mine and knows what he is speaking about

diet, a – food/meal

dingela/di'gela – wanting to join with The Number

discipline (toegekap in juries) – authority is removed/unable to use rank while an investigation takes place and a sentence is handed down to 'make you right'

dissipline nommer – when you are shown your exact role/place in the gang/busy with gang business or a gang duty

down, to – heads together for a serious discussion; to crouch down like a sangoma; the 28s raise one knee up (either right or left knee depending if the 28 is Gold or Silver Line) arms folded on the chest; the 26s and 27s crouch in a similar position but the 27s rest two fingers on the ground and the 26s down with their thumbs resting on the ground

Draad, die – the Wireless Operator (also Transistor Radio) chosen for his phenomenal memory to remember all that is said at the meetings (he walks with die Glas to ensure that a man carries out his duty – see dutied); see Ncancingolamoya/Wireless Operator/Transistor Radio

drade gegrens – an interrogation (question and answer) to protect borders

drade gebreek – end of talking and the action begins

drink – hy kan drink/he can drink/he can handle it

dronk – lustful/someone who does not think straight

dronkie/drunkard – a gang member of the 3rd Division of the 28 Gold Line who is mad for blood/aggressive

duidelik – clear/understood perfectly

dutied – a member who is issued with an instruction to commit an act (particularly of violence/stabbing) after a gang disciplinary hearing; he will be accompanied by *Die Glas en Die Draad* who will report back as to the manner in which he performed his duty

E

eight/ag – always a reference to the Camp of 28 (isispohlongo)

F

fanigalore – the term the 26s use for prison language/a mining term for the language the miners developed

fondela (see manje) – know, know that, understand that, recognise you by the signs, acknowledge the signs

Forties, the – out of action, either in solitary confinement or the hospital; from Roaring Forties, it can indicate trouble is brewing (see Mambozas)

fotcha/fotsha – see/you must see/you must wise up

fotsisa – show/cause to see

fotsisana/gefotsisana – discuss

four walls – the prison (admission/first meal/hospital/single cells)

fourth camp – the warders

frans (skone frans) – new inmate who knows nothing/uncontaminated by gang or prison ways and is potentially a gang recrtuit; a vuil frans is a prisoner who has annoyed the Number and will be targeted if a strong threat, the vuil frans may have reported on the gang or interfered and when a gang member is 'dutied' it is the vuil frans who will be stabbed (the vuil frans may be informed he is a target and persuaded not to lay a complaint, possibly through some act of bribery or a threat)

full force – coming with authority

G

gamka – to proceed from (see qamka)

gatela/gegatela – part company/go separate ways

gazi – bloed/blood

gazilams – blood brothers

gcina – keep/recognise

Gcwalisa! – Maak vol die Nommer! (Xhosa) see The Number

gebruike – goods, groceries, provisions, luxuries, drugs, anything of use

gebruike one – drugs/dagga

gebruike two – tobacco

gebruike three (see gebruike volish) – food

gebruike nommer – drugs

gebruike volish – food

gedala – dead (used in connection with fighting i.e.killing/injuring)

Germiston, The – the 28 member (Lieutenant) who allocates the privates (females)/indicates who they will be paired with (also called Amapint/Jim Crow)

gesnyde grond – claim ground or turf/when the cell or exercise yard is divided up between the three camps so that they can co-exist without having to be in direct contact

giemba – a greedy person who never gets enough, esp. of food

gif/gal (see poison) – sex in the Camp of 28

Glas, die – field glasses or binoculars/see Inspector/Mafotcha and also Draad

Goba – magistrate

Gold Line – see Bloodline (spill blood to enter)

Golia/Goliath 1 – the gang member who represents Magubaan and monitors the private line of the 28s (see Colonel's child)

grasgroen – a reference to the colours of the Camp of 28

green – a green stamp means a case is dismissed or a privilege awarded (28s)

Grey – head of the 26s (Volle Nommer Grey/a full gang member who has completed everything necessary to play his role)

grond sny/geskaal – share turf/give up some territory for the other side

gwala my/gcwala – look at me, acknowledge me, respect what I say, listen to me

gwalisela – to complete

153

H

Hawersak, Die – The Knapsack/a reference to Sgt. Two of the Gold Line who carries a rucksack full of tobacco for the wyfies in the Silver Line

heart beats (hart klop) – a reference in the 28 Camp to a heart that beats twice indicating Silver Line; a heart that beats three times or once refers to Gold Line

Hekke, Die – gates; metaphorical entry point to the gangs at initiation, there is no exit

hlathini – the metaphorical bush that the members live in prior to initiation

Hollander – a violent prisoner/always a reference to a 27 gang member

Hom! Hom! – the greeting used between 28s and 27s

Hosh! – an interjection that gets a conversation going/take note of me

Huistoe Kom, Die – (also Die Langpad) Homecoming recitation that a man learns when he is accepted into the Camp/first page of The Book

I

Inkosi Kakhulu/Nkosi Kakhulu – the Great Chief/see Nongoloza

Inspector, the – see Mafotcha

Ishumielnambini – Twelve Points

isispohlongo – eight/always a reference to the 28s (Zulu)

isithupa – six/always a reference to the 26s (Zulu)

isixhenxe – seven/always a reference to the 27s (isiXhosa)

J

Jaar, die Sesde – this refers to a Saturday which is the day that the 26 Parliament sits, it is the day that those who are 'dutied' plan to carry out their instructions and the day that the Glas and Draad go to the deep level to see if the soldiers have learned their portion of the Makhulu Book; on this day the banker who drives the caravel (small fast light ship) will report back to the gang on all that they possess in terms of wealth and will refer to his blackboard which is invisible (it's all in his head). The 27s do their work on a Sunday and the Eights get the whole weekend!

jare/jarred/years – always used in place of days (prison time passes slowly)

jarred gesny – years went by (meaning days later)

jeba – kom ons gaan/come let's go

jikijela (jigijela) – the eyes are everywhere (a 26 reference)/to investigate/eyes in the back of your head/to question closely

Jim Crow – a segregationist; see Germiston/Amapint

juries/jury – someone in 'juries' will be subjected to 'special circumstances' that prevent him, for the time being, from carrying out his role in the gang (see pp 95-6)

K

kamandela – to catch someone out (see komondela)

kammaflas – confuse someone/disorientate someone/mislead

kanna-kanna/khanda-khanda – a gun or weapon in the 28 initiation

kap hulle sterte – privileges are removed/territory removed

keep the jail alive – the 26s/their role is to get provisions for The Number

154

Kilikijan – see Ngilikityane/a corruption of the Xhosa name by Afrikaans speaking prisoners

Klip, Die – the stone on which the laws were written that sanctioned same-sex practices

klip kap – a request for sex (Kan ek jou klip kap?/Can I have sex with you?) see water and sweat

komondela – to commandeer

koppel, gekoppel en nommer speel – belong together, work together, when I see you I see myself

kraale – refers to Deep Level and stalle/seems to be mainly a ref. to 28

kring sit – a serious meeting

kroon – money

kroon, man van – a 26

kroon, gedagte van – obsessed with money/26

kroon kyk – the work of the 26s/to get their hands on money

Kruispad – see Crossroads

L

landela – to return

Langpad, Die – see Huistoe Kom

Leiland – the farm of Rabie/ also a reference to meat which is a very important part of a prisoner's diet

linkerkant (left-hand side) – always a reference to the Silver Line (female line) of the 28s/a sexual reference

Lord, the – (see pp 103-4) figureheads in the Camp of 27 and 28

lungela – a right

M

maak en doen (you cannot) – you cannot do what you want/you follow gang procedures at all times

mabobas – pipes of the Nyanga/stethoscope

Madakeni/Madagunee – the fighting general of the 26s named for the mdaka, the brass armband warn on the upper arm by high ranking members of Zulu society

Madala One – meaning the First One (see Nongoloza)/Old One with seniority

Mafotcha/Mafotsha – see Inspector, the Binoculars, die Glas

Magubaan – Nongoloza's catamite

magunyas – see ngunyas

Magielou-gielou – the Judge

make manskappe – see tambola

Makhulu Book – the Big Book that contains the oral history of The Number

Makhwezi – the Shooting Star/figurehead of the 26s, but could also be a reference to Ngilikityane

malighta/malinas – clever youngsters, franse, not in a gang yet, newcomers with (gang) potential

Mambozas – see the Forties

mampata/mpatha – (see nwata/vark skelm) a nothing/a rubbish/someone who is not respected/greenhorn/novice/ignorant/unschooled/new recruit

manje – to know (see fondela)

mapoeza – a reference to cops/warders/the farmer Rabie/anyone working against the ethos of The Number

masalon – authorised aggressive punishment/an act of discipline in which the member is beaten (the head must never be hurt or injured)

Mcobozi – the scribe (sometimes Rwenza/also Mabalang)

Meli/Mehli – the lawyer in the gang hierarchy

memeza/memenja – wait!

minute, gee – give me a second/a chance

minute, vir die – for the moment (used particularly when a 26 becomes a 27 to discuss issues with the 28s)

moeg raak – tired of/as in tired of doing your gang duty (it's dangerous to be accused of this)

Moliva, House of Moliva/Moliva Boy – a private in the Silver Line, probably a corruption of Mooi River/meaning a pretty or nice river - indicating that these members have an easy time as wyfies in prison or a *mooi lewe*; and a play on the fact that the Silver Line represents beauty/people being sexual beings

Mtshali – see Blacksmith

myne/mines, the – synonymous with prison

Mzozephi – the birth name of Nongoloza meaning 'which genealogical house do you come from?' (a name not used or even recognised by The Number)

Mzukwana Spohlongo (see umzakwaan) – the Oath of Eight/with the inference that it is an an oath that was first used outside of the prisons

N

nanje mpela – it's fine, correct, we agree it's okay

nasies (see verre lande) – the other prisons/the one in which the speaker does not reside

Ncancingolamoya – the Draad in the Camp of 28/see Draad

Ndiyaze! – maak vol die Nommer (Zulu version) – see The Number

Ngilikityane – the head of the 27s; the root of the name is *ilitye* the Xhosa word for stone and the name indicates that this is the man who moved/shoved the stone (on which gang law was written) in other words Ngilikityane challenged the laws of Nongoloza (see: Kilikijan/Jim Big Head/Ntlokonkulu/Skalaka/Ntolombom or The Arrow of Life/ The Protector)

Ngilikityane / Arrow of Life / Ntolombom/ The Protector/ Skalaka (an astonishingly speedy entrance/possibly a combination of skielik in Afrikaans and the Zulu word khalakhata meaning swift entrance) – all names for the head of the Camp of 27

Ngulugudu (corruption of Nkhulunkhulu) – the main character/hero in the 28s' version of The Crossroads; meaning the Great Chief, a special person

ngunyas – stars tattooed on the shoulders to indicate rank in the gang

nikeza – to ask or question

Nkulu Zulu – meaning Big Zulu, another name for Nongoloza once he went to jail

nobangela (from banga meaning to cause or demand) – an order/demand

nogapela – same as duidelike/all is well (used often by 28s – as in nanje mpela meaning *it is fine/correct/we agree/it is okay*)

Nogidela – leader of the dance/the teacher of soldiers in the Camp of 26 (see Blackboard)

nomakanjani die nobangela – follow orders without question no matter what the reason/outcome/danger

Nongoloza – the Giver of Rules/ Elevated One founder of The Number and the head of the 28s see Nkulu Zulu/Madala One/Inkosi Kakhulu; before entering prison he was known as Mzozephi Mathebula and later he took the name of Jan Note (the last two names are unknown to The Number in prison)

Nozala – parental figurehead in the Silver Line of the Camp of 28

Ntlokonkulu – see Ngilikityane

Ntolombom – Arrow of Life/Arrow of Blood/Protector; the name Ngilikityane is known by in prison (see: Ngilikityane); it implies protection; the role of the 27s (whose leader was Ngilikityane) is to see that gang protocol is followed so that gang boundaries are not infringed and the separate territories remain inviolate; the 27s are guardians of the gang laws and peacekeepers between the 26s and 28s

ntshontsho – a small fry, chicken, spy

Ntshotshisane – the Colonel in the 28s who holds the invisible position of the spy.

Number, The (Die Nommer) – a generic name for the Number Gangs in prison; previously known as The Ninevites and the Regiment of the Hills (Umkosi wa Ntaba), Amalitas or People of the Stone, names no longer in use; but the term Nongolozas (for those on the fringes of the gang), which was used particularly for bands of vagrants roaming outside prison in the early years when The Ninevites operated outside of prison, is still used; there are several important slogans that indicate the cult status of The Number e.g. die Nommer sal jou wys – the Number will punish you; lyn van die Nommer; opspeel met lyn van Nommer meaning do it as the Number prescribes, or proceed as the Number prescribes, or in the tradition of the Number; as well as *Maak vol die Nommer!* as in complete the work of The Number, cleanse The Number, full power to The Number

Number Ones – unarmed privates in the Camp of 26

Number Twos – officers in the Camp of 26

nwatas – wrongs (against gang) see mampata

nwata balisa/nwatas praat – talk rubbish/crap/lies

nyanga/nyangi – a traditional African doctor

nzulu – inside/deep inside the gang or mine

O

ou met 'n kantoor – gang member with a ranking position

ouens – gang brothers

P

Pawule Mambazo – hero in the 26s' version of The Crossroads (also called Paul or Po) and the name is indicative of someone with special attributes

pen (wit/swart) – implies presence of the special book/the brain

perd,'n – (a horse) a warder who smuggles drugs for the gang

phakamisa/pakamiesa – rise up/confirm/upwardly mobile moment for that Camp/ agree/all goes according to the Number/exalt/elevate

phakamisa chaisana – it's fine/in order/correct

phakamisa phezulu – raise up

Phambuka Songaqo – see Crossroads

phela/pela – correct/as in agree (Nommer is pela – the Number is correct)

phezula/gephezula/phenzula – take in/take in deep (as in 'deep into the Number')/ take someone to a place/to go to steal something

piemp – spy

pikelela/phikelela – sent/go to/went/persist

Plank, die – see skombizo

plough – see skoffel

Points, The – a reference to the Four Points or Twelve Points which operate like parliaments or courts of law

poison (see gif) – can be a reference to sex /met poison of salute; used by the 26s to indicate something is either done badly (met poison) or properly (met salute)

Private Line (28s) – the division in the Silver Line from which the wyfies are selected

Protector, The – see Ngilikityane

Q

qamka – to proceed from/go on from

queen – a reference to the wife of Rabie

Queen's Bed – the corner of the cell closed off with sheets behind which the 28s complete their rituals/a term only used by the Silver Line

R

Rabie – the farmer who persecuted his workmen and let his bull, Rooiland, gore them

Rantsoen Jaar – means ration day and is the word the 28s use for a Friday when the orders are rationed out amongst the gang; the 28s are allocated two days for their tasks, the Saturday is duty day and Sunday they initiate gang members

red/rooi – indicates violence/blood e.g. sy gedagte is rooi/a person committed to violence/red stamp at The Points indicates blood will flow/thin red line indicates fighting in the Camp of 26

regtekant – the right side/a reference to the work of the 26s/27s (see right-side)

respek en dissipline – done with respect and discipline/in the correct manner for the Number

right-hand (side) – on the side of sexual purity, the side the 26s select because they do not promote same-sex activities (as opposed to left-hand side which means sexual activity in the Camp of 28); Gold Line in the 28s also use the term *right side* as they are dominant in the sexual relationship

righting a wrong – one may be dutied to stab a warder to prove dominance and to rise in rank, or to correct a mistake made which weakened the gang in the eyes of others in prison

Rooiland – the bull of Rabie that was slaughtered/a reference to meat

S

sabela, salazisa, shalambom, fanigalore – prison language – used between gang members only; when gang issues are discussed in a coded language that only gang members may use; no frans may speak this language as the members are given the *special information and thoughts* that go with the language and that authorise the members to sabela with true undertanding

Salute! – all is correct/well

Salute! Salute! – greeting used amongst 28 and 26 gang members

salute – a peaceful gang greeting when there is no conflict or unfinished business but also: Salute aan Nommer (honour The Number); die wat salute het - good stuff; that which does not bring trouble to the Camp

Scotlanders, The – another name for the 26s (perhaps because of their love of money!)

Secret, the – what the 28s are busy with/if the secret is revealed they have nothing left

seun – a reference to the non-dominant partner in the 28s/see wyfie

sfogiso – a warning (from siboniso)

shebanga – blanket

short-arms – when the Camp/Gang is in mourning for a dead brother

Shotgun, The – the One-time Shotgun opens The Points/the Two-time Shotgun gives the Nyanga/Doctor permission to proceed

Sif, die/Sieve – the General in the 28s who issues the knife when a man must do a duty

sikhosi – the chiefs in the gang/senior gang members

Silver Line – a division of the 28 gang; those who enter from the left-hand side; named after Joseph Silver a notorious pimp in Johannesburg in the 1890s/also known as the Female or Private Line

sitha/gesitha – sit/seated

sixhenxe/sewe – (meaning seven) always a reference to the 27s

Skalaka – see Ngilikityane

skangaka (kangaka) – be there/be present/on guard/also used to call someone as in 'come over here'

skarra – to scavenge (again a 26 reference)

skelm sleutel – this opens the door to non-legitimate activities (a term used frequently by the 26s who rob with a clear conscience)

skiet (a reference to a stabbing, not shooting) – as in *hy het sy rank afgeskiet*/he drew blood to get his rank (the Inspector, for example, always draws blood to get rank)

skietyster – a knife

skoemba (from isikhumba) – the skin of Rooiland on which the laws were imprinted

skoffel die grond met bloed – a reference to re-opening the Gold Line or Bloodline of the 28s at prisons when it has been suspended/ploughing with blood/taking warder blood

skombizo (from yisikhombisa - 27 in Zulu) – twenty-seven; if someone comes from skombizo he has permission to stab (used to refer to Captain of the Blood with six stars also known as Die Plank)

skool gee – teach gang procedures

skoon dedagtes – clear conscience or clean conscience; always a reference to a 26 who has robbed via manipulation and not violence; a specialist in taking someone hostage emotionally and making one feel guilty if what is asked for is not provided

skoon skiet/as in 'die land skoonskiet' or 'skiet die berge oop' – when all three gangs combine to confront prison authorities (as in rioting/attacking staff) because they feel the warders have denied them their rights, have interfered with gang activities, are too tough on them or a task team has been called in to remove drugs and weapons; *skoon skiet* can make the prisons ungovernable; this occurs in daylight hours because at night they are locked in, the Draad van Holland (a 27) will stab when the sun rises and then the Draad van 28 stabs and then the Draad van 26; it also means *to right a wrong*

skoot (het gelandêla) – the drugs have arrived

slasluka/slasluka daleka – is a reference to work (of a bad kind) that completes, justifies, honours or strengthens The Number

Sontop! – salute of the 26s

Sontop, ouens van – the 26s

spanga – astonish (*to meet in the spanga* means that during exercise time the gang has planned to stab someone)

special book – the brain/memory

spohlongo (as in sweer van spohlongo) – the Oath of Eight

staan op! – is always an order to fight

Stairs, the – another name for the Governor General/Silver Line/Div.One because he can go up to the Twelve Points

stalala – I call myself/ I style myself

stalle – similar in meaning to Deep Level or kraal

stam – the mark of the gang

sterkbene – have the guts/strength for gang business

sterkmaak – strengthen for gang work

stimela – a reference to a new arrival, a ranking gang member who has just been transferred from another prison

stokkies – awaiting trial lock-up/quarantine

Stone, The – see Klip/the rules for the gang were inscribed on the stone and, according to the 28s, included same-sex practices

stongas – wrongs

stupa (isithupa) – a six /26

suleka – arrive

sun (son), sunrise, sononder – there are frequent references to the sun as the 26s work by day and the 28s by night when the sun sets; sunrise indicates the 26s take control and when it is *sononder* their day's work ends; sien nie son nie (never sees the sun) is a reference to the Gold Line of the 28s who defend the camp/Gates of Sunrise refers to the entry point into the 26 Camp

swaar maar ook lekker – a reference to the work of 26 (hard but nice)

swart – this indicates wrong things done/wrong thinking/not in accord with gang beliefs or actions

sweat – wiping sweat from the brow/a reference to sex having taken place (see klip kap and water)

T

tak veertig – dagga

tambola – to make manskappe/to initiate new 28s

Tambuka, Die – a corruption of Phambuka Songaqo (see Crossroads)

tennis – a derogatory terms used by all gangs/means playing around, not taking it seriously/ reference to female work or to someone not in any Camp/some 28s refer to Nongoloza and Ngilikityane watching Rabie's women play tennis over the fence/ 26s (who were in prison) know nothing about any tennis match

toegekap in juries (see discipline) – not able to go about usual activities

tola – to hear/listen

tolomhlophe – to find the white person within yourself; this is idiomatic, it means an impossible task is given that renders you helpless or ineffectual as the goal cannot be attained; it's also used as a reference to the Silver Two who may not have sex in his camp but only outside the camp

Transistor Radio – see Draad

Twalfpunt, Die – full senior gang council of six members

U

Umfailand – the Colonel in the 28s who keeps the skin of Rooiland on which the rules are written

umkhosi – a chief/senior gang member (Umkhosi – the Lord)

umzakwaan, die – meaning one small moment in time and a reference to the world outside of prison which the gang member has left behind him

V

vark skelm – a pig/a rubbish (see mampata)

vasgebrand in die bomvana – the genuine article (when a member stabs to get his rank)

vedala – it's over/ finished/ he is weakened/aged/ hurt/dead

161

Vedala die Nommer! – see The Number (the Number has completed its work)

vedala saam – suffer/die together/finish together

veertig/the forties – the term applied to a new arrival from another prison who is placed in *skoon juries van sake* until he can give proof that he has not offended gang laws at the previous prison (if he has broken gang law he will not be able to fulfil his rank until he had cleansed himself by carrying out a specific duty)

verre lande – see nasies

vierde oog (fourth eye) – be on the lookout for danger

visinteer – to search

vleis – a weapon (a man van bloed en vleis/an armed man); used in context: *Generaal met vleis en bloed from Grey se kant as Holland* - the 27 who negotiates with the 28s on behalf of the 26s when they meet at the Crossroads/Walcross

voetspore doodmaak – cover tracks

voleish three – food

vuilwerk – the work of those who report on gang actions to the authorities

W

walcross – the name given to the daily meeting and report back of the three gangs

water dries up – the wyfie is removed/sexual partner leaves

water/water spouting – a reference to sex (see klip kap)

werk/work – werk is *bitter en swaar* (28 work); werk is *swaar maar ook lekker*(26 work); *dag en nag te werke met bloed* (27 work)

werk soek – apply for gang membership

wetslaaners – human rights activists/the gangs believe that they were formed as a group to fight for the rights of prisoners

white/wit – all is correct (26s); as in pure white position/spier wit post/means a position in the Camp of 26 – pure, without any same-sex practices; also the probationer's stamp in the Camp of 28

Wireless Operator – see Draad

witbene – the dead

wyfie – (meaning little wife) derogatory term for probationers in the Silver Line of the 28s (should not be used in discussion with a 28)

wysraak/wysmaak/raak wys – empower/inform/school someone